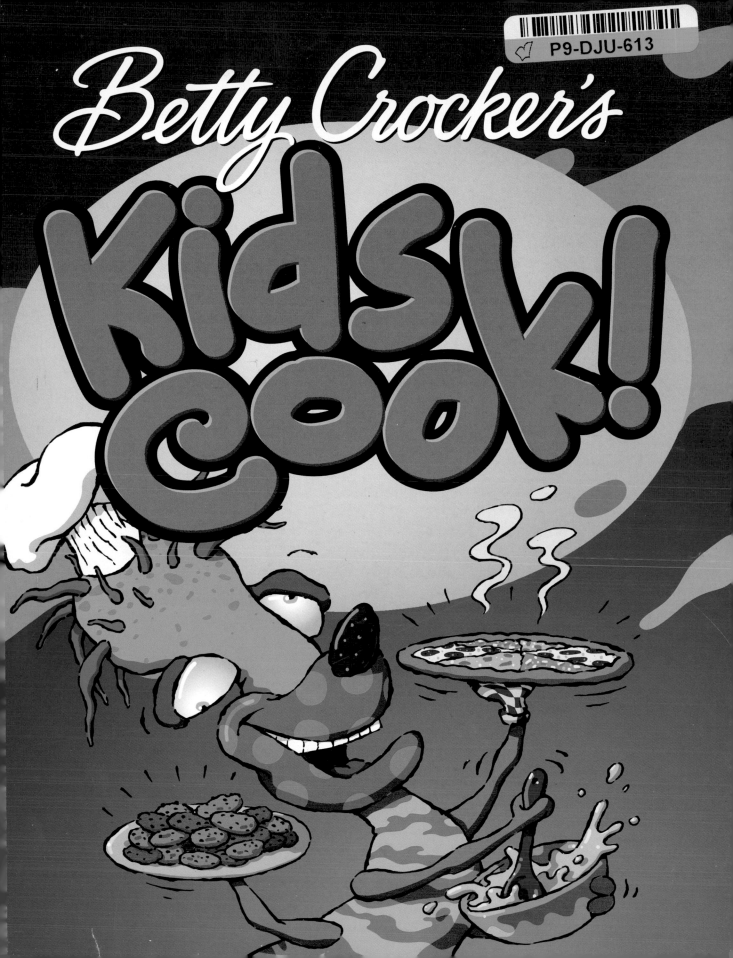

MACMILLAN GENERAL REFERENCE USA
A Pearson Education Macmillan Company
1633 Broadway
New York, NY 10019-6785

Macmillan Publishing books may be purchased for business or sales promotional use. For information please write: Special Markets Department, Macmillan Publishing USA, 1633 Broadway, New York, NY 10019.

Crocker, Betty.
    Betty Crocker's Kids Cook! — 1st ed.
        p.   cm.
    Includes index.
    ISBN 0-02-863406-3
        1. Cookery Juvenile literature.   [1.Cookery.]   I. Title.
    II. Title: Kids cook!
    TX714.C756 1999
    641.5'123—dc21

                                                    99-40460
                                                    CIP

GENERAL MILLS, INC.
Betty Crocker Kitchens
Manager, Publishing: Lois L. Tlusty
Editor: Kelly Kilen
Recipe Development: Betty Crocker Kitchens Home Economists
Food Stylists: Delores Custer, Lisa Homa
Nutritionist: Nancy Holmes, R.D.

For consistent baking results, the Betty Crocker Kitchens recommend Gold Medal Flour.

Manufactured in China
10 9 8 7 6 5 4 3 2 1
First Edition

Photographic Services
Art Director: Scott Meola
Photographer: Nora Scarlett
Cover Design: Paul Costello
Interior Design: Scott Meola
Illustrator: Dennas Davis
Cover Illustration: Dennas Davis

Contents

HEY KIDS—

Come on out here to the kitchen and let's get cooking! Got the munchies? Whip up a batch of chocolate chip cookies or make a pizza just the way you like it. Want to slurp a frosty shake or dig into a messy, delicious taco? Then you've come to the right place—it's all in here.

This book was made just for you! It's crammed with mouthwatering recipes and other cooking stuff you need to know to be a fabulous cook. Check out the recipes—they're a cinch to follow and there's a picture on every page. I've also packed the book with great tips and thrown in a couple of recipe twists, in case you are feeling extra adventurous. And your parents can chill out—kids just like you tried every recipe to be sure they really work and taste great. That means they'll be sure to work in your kitchen too!

Cooking is cool—especially when you know how to make the foods you love to eat. So, open the book, pick something delicious, and dig in!

Betty Crocker

P.S. Have a blast!

Cook's Corner

What could be more fun than cooking up a mouthwatering, lip-smackin', downright delicious dish? Get your creative cooking juices flowing, and let your taste buds tango. You're about to blast off to a whole new world of cooking and baking adventures. But wait! Before you chop, measure, blend and stir, turn the page and check out the Top 10 list for the kitchen.

TOP 10 KITCHEN TIPS

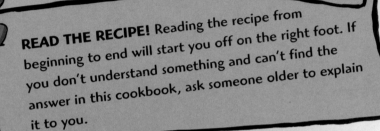

1 **PICK AND TELL!** Set aside some time to pick out a recipe you want to make. If your recipe uses the stove or oven or a sharp object such as a knife or vegetable peeler, tell an adult in case you need a helping hand.

2 **READ THE RECIPE!** Reading the recipe from beginning to end will start you off on the right foot. If you don't understand something and can't find the answer in this cookbook, ask someone older to explain it to you.

3 **STAY SAFE!** You'll find some important safety pointers on pages 8–11. It's a good idea to read these tips and be sure you understand them before starting to cook.

4 **LOOK FOR THE LISTS!** At the start of each recipe, the stuff you need is listed in the order it's used in the recipe. These lists will help you organize all of your ingredients and utensils. Be sure you have all the ingredients you need before starting to cook. If not, check with the shopper in your family and add the ingredients to his or her list—you can even offer to go and help with the shopping!

5 **BECOME A MASTER AT MEASURING!** You don't need any magic powers or mega math skills to measure. All you need are a couple of tips (see pages 17–20) and a steady hand.

TAKE IT ONE STEP AT A TIME! Following the recipe step by step will keep you from losing your place and skipping anything important. It's also a good idea to finish one step before you start the next.

DO A RECIPE REVIEW! Reread the recipe to make sure that you haven't left anything out. Here's a little trick: Before you start cooking, put everything you need on a tray. When the tray is empty, you'll know you haven't left anything out!

CLEAN UP AS YOU GO—it makes less work at the end! When you finish using a utensil (except for sharp knives), put it in warm, soapy water to soak. It's best to wash sharp knives one by one so you don't reach your hand into the soapy water and accidentally cut yourself on the sharp blades.

MAKE A CLEAN FINISH! Everyone dreads doing dishes, but cleanup is the coolest way to keep the kitchen looking spic and span. So, wash and dry all the utensils you have used, or put them in the dishwasher. Don't forget to wash the counters, and wipe off the table, too.

DOUBLE CHECK! When you're all done cooking, check the stove, oven and any other appliances to be sure you have turned them off. Put away any appliances you have used so they'll be ready for the next time you're in the kitchen.

The kitchen is the place to be! But it also can be a little bit tricky and risky, unless you know the ropes. Here are some important pointers to help keep you safe in the kitchen:

Come Clean!

- Before you start, wash your hands with lots of warm, soapy water. Make sure you dry them really well so you don't have slippery fingers.

- Pick out an apron, and throw it on so you don't get spills and splashes all over your clothes. If you have a shirt with long sleeves, roll them up. If your hair is long, tie it back so it won't get in the way while you're cooking.

- Keep counters and floors dry and free of slippery spots by wiping up spills as they happen. A roll of paper towels and a damp dishcloth can come in handy for when a quick wipe up is needed.

Chop! Chop!

- Check in before you chop it up! If your recipe uses a sharp knife or can opener, it's a good idea to check with someone older so he or she can answer any questions or help out if you need it.

- When cutting or chopping ingredients, use a cutting board so you don't cut the counter. Turn the sharp edge of a knife or vegetable peeler away from you and your hand when you chop or peel foods so you don't cut yourself.

Mix It Up!

- Whenever you put the beaters in or take them out of an electric mixer, make sure you first turn off the mixer and unplug it. It's also **VERY IMPORTANT** that you don't use any electrical appliance near water or have wet hands when using one.

- Before you scrape the side of a bowl or container, turn off the electric mixer so the rubber scraper won't get caught in the blades.

Hot Pots!

- If you're about to touch something that's hot, grab that pot holder first! This is especially important when you are taking things out of the oven or microwave or when you are cooking food on the stove. Pick out pot holders that are thick and dry, so you don't burn yourself.

- Pot handles can accidentally get bumped if they are sticking out over the edge of the stove. If you turn the handles so that they are pointed toward the center of the stove, you'll keep pots from getting knocked off the stove and spilling hot food.

- Spoons that are made of all metal can get very hot and can burn your fingers. If you are stirring something on the stove, use a wooden spoon or a long-handled spoon with a wooden or plastic handle.

- Use a tight-fitting lid or aluminum foil when a recipe says to cover something on the stove or in the oven. When you lift the lid off a pot, make sure you tip it away from you. That way, you'll keep your face away from steam that could burn you.

- Cook your food, not the counter! Hot pots and pans can ruin the countertop, so give them a resting place on a wire cooling rack or a pot holder.

In and Out of the Oven

- Check your recipe before you turn on the oven to see if the oven racks need to be moved higher or lower. It's much easier and safer to move the racks when the oven is cold, not sizzling hot.

- If you're putting more than one pan in the oven, check to make sure that you don't put one pan directly over another on the two oven racks. If the pans aren't stacked, all the food will cook the same way and for the same amount of time.

- When you put pans into and take pans out of the oven and when you check to see if a recipe is done, you might want to ask an adult for help. Also, if you need to take a peek, close the oven door quickly so you keep the oven hot.

9

Microwave Musts

- Read the instruction book for your microwave oven to find out the kinds of foods it cooks best and the right cooking times.

- Some containers, such as those made of aluminum foil or metal, can cause sparks in the microwave, so be sure not to use them. Instead, find microwave-safe dishes and utensil in your kitchen to use. If you're unsure which dishes can go in the microwave, ask an adult helper.

- Read the recipe to check if the food should be covered when you put it in the microwave. A sheet of waxed paper makes a good cover for microwave-safe containers so food doesn't spatter.

- Food heated in the microwave can make the container it's in very hot, so be careful when you take a dish out of the microwave.

- After you take a dish out of the microwave, let it cool on the counter for a few minutes because it may have some hot spots that could burn your mouth if you eat it right away.

STAY IN THE FOOD SAFETY ZONE

Keeping food safe to eat is easy if you stay in the safety zone—the *food safety* zone, that is. Remember tips one, two, three, and you'll be home free!

 Keep it clean!

- Raw eggs, chicken, turkey, meat and fish can carry harmful bacteria that are not destroyed until the food is cooked. If you're cutting raw chicken or turkey, meat or fish, use a plastic cutting board. Be sure to wash the cutting board—and your hands—with lots of warm, soapy water when you're done. Don't cut anything else on the cutting board until you've washed it well, so you don't contaminate other fresh foods that might not be getting cooked at all, such as fruits and veggies.

- After using a plate for raw chicken, turkey, meat or fish, do not serve the cooked meat on the same unwashed plate. Wash it in hot, soapy water, or use a clean plate.

- After touching any raw foods, especially raw chicken, turkey, meat, fish or eggs, wash your hands with lots of warm, soapy water. Use paper towels to wipe up any spills. Then wash the counter with more warm, soapy water.

- Wash fresh fruits and vegetables in cool water, and pat them dry with paper towels before you eat them or chop them up to use in a recipe.

- Sometimes a food will look or smell bad and should be thrown out. But looks can be deceiving. Some foods may look, smell and taste okay but may actually be spoiled. If in doubt, don't taste it, and ask an adult if it should be thrown out!

2 If it's hot, keep it hot!

- Once food has been cooked, keep it hot until you're ready to serve it. If you are not going to be serving the food right away, refrigerate it as soon as possible so it stays safe to eat.

3 If it's cold, keep it cold!

- Food that is supposed to be cold should be kept in the refrigerator or freezer. Don't let frozen food thaw on the counter. If it needs to be thawed, put it in the refrigerator.

LEARN THE LANGUAGE

When you read a recipe for the first time, you may run into a word or two you don't understand. Use this list to look up any words that are particularly puzzling.

BAKE: Cook food in the oven.

BEAT: Make a mixture smooth by stirring fast with a fork, wire whisk, eggbeater or electric mixer.

BOIL: Cook a liquid in a saucepan on top of the stove until big bubbles keep rising and breaking on the surface.

BROWN: Cook food until it looks brown on the outside.

CHILL: Put food in the refrigerator until it is cold.

CHOP: Cut food into small pieces on a cutting board, using a sharp knife. Don't worry if the pieces aren't the same shape, but they should be about the same size.

COOL: Put food on the counter (usually on a wire cooling rack) until it is no longer warm when you touch it. This is especially important if you are frosting or decorating a cake or a batch of cookies. If you don't wait until the cake or cookies are completely cool, the frosting may start to melt.

COVER: Put a lid, aluminum foil or plastic wrap over food. When you cook food on the stove, use a lid. When you put food in the oven, use aluminum foil. When you put food on the counter, in the refrigerator or in the freezer, use plastic wrap or aluminum foil.

DRAIN: Pour off liquid or let it run off through the holes in a strainer or colander (see page 16). You do this to drain the water after you cook pasta or to drain the fat after you cook ground beef.

FREEZE: Put food in the freezer until it is frozen and hard as a rock.

GRATE: Rub an ingredient against the smallest holes on a grater to cut it into very small pieces.

GREASE: Spread the bottom and sides of a pan with shortening, margarine or butter, using a pastry brush or paper towel. You also can use cooking spray, which comes in a can. By greasing a pan, you will keep food from sticking to it.

KNEAD: Curve your fingers around and fold dough toward you, then push it away with the heels of your hands, using a quick rocking motion (see page 15). Kneading makes a dough smooth and stretchy.

MELT: Put a solid ingredient, such as chocolate or butter, in a saucepan and turn it into a liquid by heating it on the stove. You also can put the ingredient in a microwavable bowl and heat it in the microwave oven until melted.

MIX: Stir ingredients with a spoon, fork, eggbeater, wire whisk or electric mixer until smooth or almost smooth.

PEEL: Cut off the outer skin of fruits or vegetables, using a vegetable peeler or small sharp knife. Some fruit, such as oranges and bananas, you can peel with your fingers.

ROLL: Press a ball of dough into a flat rectangle or circle, using a rolling pin.

SHRED: Rub an ingredient against the big holes on a grater to cut it into long, skinny pieces.

SLICE: Starting at one end, cut food into flat, skinny pieces on a cutting board, using a sharp knife. The pieces should all be about the same thickness.

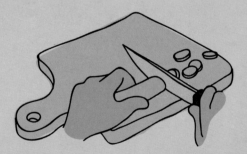

STIR-FRY: Cook food quickly in a small amount of oil over high heat, stirring all the time.

TOSS: Mix ingredients by lifting them with two spoons or forks and letting them drop back into the bowl. You do this when you make a "tossed salad."

MASTER THE METHOD

Just like roller blading or playing the piano, cooking takes a little practice to become good at it. Here are some helpful how-to's so you can polish up your cooking skills.

Crack an egg

BE SURE TO HOLD ON TO THE SLIPPERY SHELL!

Crack the egg on side of the bowl. Open the shell, letting egg fall into bowl.

Separate an egg

SOMETIMES YOU ONLY NEED THE YOLK OR THE WHITE, SO SPLIT 'EM UP.

Crack the egg on side of the bowl. Open the shell, letting yolk fall into center of the egg separator. The white will slip through the slots of the separator into the bowl. Do not separate an egg by passing the yolk back and forth from shell half to shell half because there could be bacteria in the shell, which could spoil the egg.

Knead dough

YOU WON'T "KNEAD" A WORKOUT AFTER YOU DO THIS A FEW TIMES.

 Curve your fingers around and fold dough toward you.

Push the dough away with the heels of your hands, using a quick rocking motion. The dough should look smooth and stretchy when you're done.

Take a cake out of a pan

SOMETIMES IT'S HARD TO TELL IF THE CAKE IS RIGHTSIDE UP OR UPSIDE DOWN!

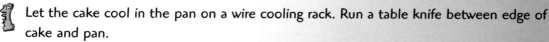

Let the cake cool in the pan on a wire cooling rack. Run a table knife between edge of cake and pan.

Cover a second wire cooling rack with waxed paper or a clean kitchen towel. Put wire rack over pan. Hold onto wire racks with both hands, and turn upside down.

Take off the pan.

Put a wire cooling rack over bottom of cake. Turn upside down again. Take off top rack. Peel off waxed paper.

Test for doneness

IS IT READY YET? TEST IT AND FIND OUT.

Poke a toothpick in the center. The toothpick should be clean when you pull it out.

Drain ground beef after cooking

. . .BUT DON'T POUR THE FAT DOWN YOUR KITCHEN DRAIN. PUT IT IN A CONTAINER AND THROW IT AWAY.

Put a strainer over a small bowl. Spoon beef into strainer to drain the fat.

Drain pasta after cooking

HANG ONTO THE HANDLE AND DON'T FORGET A POT HOLDER!

Put a colander in the sink. Pour the pasta into the colander over the sink to drain the water.

MEASURE UP

The secret to successful cooking is measuring correctly. Not all ingredients are measured the same way or with the same kind of cups or spoons. Here are some tips to help you out.

LIQUID INGREDIENTS

Use see-through measuring cups to measure liquids, such as milk or water. These cups are usually made of glass and have a spout for pouring and marks on the sides that show you how much liquid you have in the cup.

To Measure: Put the cup on the counter. Pour in some of the liquid. Bend down or stand on your tiptoes so your eye is level with the marking on the cup to check if you've poured in the right amount. If it's too much, pour a little out. If it's not enough, add a little more and check again. If you are measuring a sticky ingredient, such as honey or corn syrup, spray the cup with a little cooking spray before pouring in the ingredient. The liquid will slide right out!

If you are measuring small amounts of a liquid ingredient, such as vanilla, use a measuring spoon. These special spoons come in sets with different sizes and should be used instead of the spoons that you eat with.

DRY INGREDIENTS

Dry ingredients, such as flour, powdered sugar, granulated sugar and Bisquick® baking mix, are measured with a set of cups that stack inside one another and are made of metal or plastic.

To Measure: Choose the cup size that is listed in the recipe. Fill the cup to the top (or little bit higher), using a large spoon. Don't shake the cup or pack the ingredient into the cup. Hold the cup over a bowl or container, then scrape a metal spatula across the top (or use the flat edge of a table knife). When you're finished, the ingredient should be level with the top of the cup.

You can do the same thing with measuring spoons if you are measuring small amounts of a dry ingredient, such as baking powder, baking soda, salt or spices. Dip the measuring spoon into the ingredient to fill it. Scrape a small metal spatula across the top so the ingredient is level with the top of the spoon.

WHAT ABOUT . . . ?

Brown Sugar: Spoon brown sugar into a metal or plastic measuring cup, and press down firmly with the back of the spoon. Keep adding brown sugar until it reaches the top of the measuring cup. Scrape a metal spatula across the top so brown sugar is level with the top of the cup.

Margarine or Butter: Cut off the amount you need with a table knife. You can use the measurement marks on the wrapper as your guide. One stick of margarine or butter equals 1/2 cup; half a stick is 1/4 cup. You also can use a metal or plastic measuring cup to measure soft margarine or butter if you don't have a wrapper with measurement marks.

Shortening and Peanut Butter: Fill a plastic or metal measuring cup, using a spoon or rubber scraper. When the cup is full, scrape a metal spatula across the top. Take the shortening or peanut butter out of the cup by running a rubber scraper around the inside of the cup.

Other Stuff such as chopped nuts, chocolate chips, shredded cheese and chopped veggies can be measured in plastic or metal measuring cups. Spoon the ingredient into the cup until it reaches the top, but don't press down.

DO THE MATH

What's different, but the same? All these measurements! In our recipes, we have used the larger measurement—1/4 cup, not 4 tablespoons—but this chart will help you out for the other measuring you do in the kitchen.

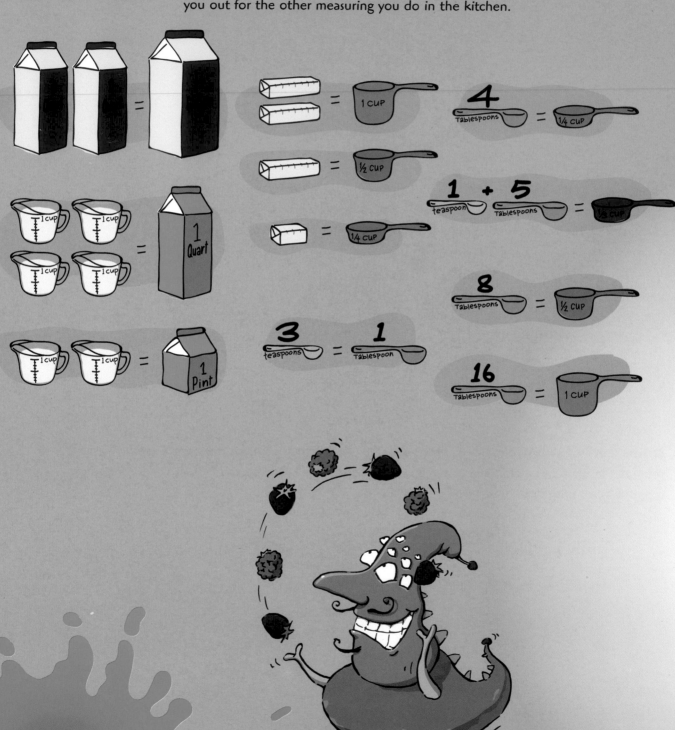

SET THE TABLE

Show off your kitchen creations by setting a great-looking table. First, count how many people you'll be serving. Then set a place for each of them at the table. For each person, put a plate on the table in front of each chair. Put a fork to the left of the plate and a knife and spoon to the right. Put a glass just above the knife, and tuck a napkin under the fork. Follow the picture below—it's that easy!

P.S. Remember to pass the dishes of food to the person on your right.

LEND A HAND (for the Cook's Adult Helper)

Kids love to cook! Making food for themselves and their family or friends can be a tasty and satisfying activity. Chances are if kids have made it themselves, they will be more likely to eat it. To ensure that a kid plus cooking in the kitchen doesn't equal a recipe for disaster, help your young chef pick out recipes that match his or her tastes and abilities, and be available to answer any questions that pop up. Kids also learn by example, and the best example is you. Show kids the right way to set the controls on the stove, oven and any other appliances. Help them out by showing them safe food-preparation techniques and how to handle hot foods and sharp objects. And most importantly, **HAVE FUN!**

ARF!

PRESENTING OUR PANEL OF EXPERTS

Meet our tried and true testers—they're kids just like you! Not only have they tested and tasted all of the recipes, they've stamped them with their seal of approval, so you know the recipes will be easy to make and taste great!

23

CHAPTER 1

Breakfast Anytime!

Where's it at?

BREAKFAST

Fabulous French "Toast" "Stix"

UTENSILS

Cutting board
Serrated knife
Rectangular baking dish,
   13 x 9 inches
Medium mixing bowl
Measuring cups
Eggbeater or fork
Pancake turner
Plastic bag with zipper top
Rolling pin
Pie plate or
   shallow dish
Large skillet

INGREDIENTS

4 slices bread
3 eggs
1/4 cup milk
2 cups cornflakes cereal
1 tablespoon margarine or butter
Maple-flavored syrup or your
   favorite pancake topping,
   if you like

26

CHECK IT OUT!

Bread that is a little dry makes fantastic French toast! You may want to try French or Italian bread, which aren't as soft and squishy as regular white bread.

1 Cut each slice of **BREAD** into 3 strips on the cutting board, using the knife. Put bread strips in the baking dish.

2 Crack the **EGGS** on side of the bowl, letting eggs slip into bowl. Add the **MILK** to eggs. Beat with the eggbeater or fork until eggs look foamy. Pour over bread strips. Turn bread strips over, using the pancake turner, to coat other sides.

3 Put the **CEREAL** in the plastic bag. Seal bag closed. Use the rolling pin to crush cereal. Dump crushed cereal into the pie plate or shallow dish.

5 Take the bread strips out of egg mixture, and dip it into crushed cereal. Turn bread strips over, using the pancake turner, to coat other sides.

6 Put the cereal-coated bread in heated skillet. Cook for about 4 minutes or until bottoms of bread strips are golden brown (you can lift an edge with the pancake turner and peek). Turn bread over. Cook on other sides for about 4 minutes or until bottoms are golden brown.

7 Serve with the **SYRUP** or **PANCAKE TOPPING**, if you like

I sprinkled my French toast with cinnamon and sugar.
—BEN

4 Put the **MARGARINE** in the skillet. Heat over medium heat until margarine is melted (you can tilt the skillet so inside of skillet will be coated with margarine).

NUTRITION INFORMATION

1 SERVING (3 "STIX"): Calories 205 (Calories from Fat 70); Fat 8g (Saturated 2g); Cholesterol 160mg; Sodium 380mg; Carbohydrate 26g (Dietary Fiber 1g); Protein 8g

% DAILY VALUE: Vitamin A 20%; Vitamin C 6%; Calcium 6%; Iron 30%

DIET EXCHANGES: 2 Starch, 1 Fat

Prep: Cook: Makes:

20 minutes **5** minutes **18** pancakes

Squeeze & Scribble Pancakes

iNGReDieNTS

Shortening (to grease griddle)
2 eggs
2 cups Bisquick Original baking mix
1 cup milk
SHOWSTOPPER STRAWBERRY TOPPING or **PEANUT BUTTER MAPLE-SYRUP** (pages 30–31), if you like

UTeNSiLS

Griddle or electric skillet
Pastry brush
Measuring cups
Medium mixing bowl
Fork
Spoon
Plastic squeeze bottle
   with narrow opening
28 Pancake turner

Here's another idea

Make **PERFECTLY PLAIN PANCAKES:** Instead of pouring the batter into the squeeze bottle, pour about 1/4 cup of the batter from a measuring cup onto the hot griddle to make each round pancake.

1 Heat the griddle over medium heat, or heat electric skillet to 375°. (To test griddle or skillet, sprinkle with a few drops of water. If bubbles jump around, heat is just right.)

2 Grease the heated griddle with the **SHORTENING**, using the pastry brush.

3 Crack the **EGGS** on side of the bowl, letting eggs slip into bowl. Add the **BAKING MIX** and **MILK** to eggs. Beat with the fork until mixture is smooth.

4 Spoon about 1/2 cup of the batter into the squeeze bottle. Squeeze batter from bottle onto hot griddle to form a letter. (You must make the letter backward on the griddle so it will appear the right way when pancakes are served!) When bottom side of letter is golden brown, pour 1/4 cup of the batter from a measuring cup in a circle over letter to make a round pancake.

5 Cook about 2 minutes longer or until edges of the pancakes are golden brown and slightly dry. Turn the pancakes over, using the pancake turner. Cook for about 2 minutes or until bottoms of the pancakes are golden brown.

6 Serve the pancakes with **SHOWSTOPPER STRAWBERRY TOPPING** or **PEANUT BUTTER MAPLE-SYRUP**, if you like.

CHECK IT OUT!

Leave out the lumps! Pancake batter must be smooth so it can be squeezed out of the bottle. If the tip gets stuck with batter, use a toothpick to clean out the opening.

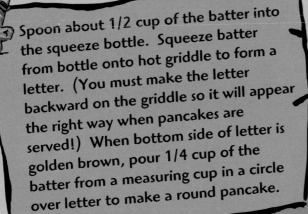

NUTRITION INFORMATION

1 SERVING (3 PANCAKES): Calories 200 (Calories from Fat 70); Fat 8g (Saturated 2g); Cholesterol 75mg; Sodium 610mg; Carbohydrate 26g (Dietary Fiber 0g); Protein 6g

% DAILY VALUE: Vitamin A 4%; Vitamin C 0%; Calcium 12%; Iron 8%

DIET EXCHANGES: 1 1/2 Starch, 2 Fat

UTeNSiLS

Measuring cup
Colander
Paper towels
Cutting board
Small sharp knife
Measuring spoons
Medium saucepan
Wooden spoon

iNGReDieNTS

1 cup fresh or frozen strawberries
1 jar (12 ounces) strawberry jam
2 tablespoons margarine or butter
2 tablespoons water

Showstopper Strawberry Topping

Here's another idea

For another top-notch pancake topper, make **PEANUT BUTTER-MAPLE SYRUP**: Put 1 cup maple-flavored syrup and 3 tablespoons creamy peanut butter in a saucepan. Stir with a wooden spoon until mixed. Cook mixture over medium heat, stirring all the time, until syrup is smooth and bubbly.

1 If using fresh strawberries, put the **STRAWBERRIES** in the colander. Rinse strawberries with cold water. Pat dry with the paper towels.

2 Remove the stems from strawberries. Cut each strawberry into 4 pieces on the cutting board, using the knife.

3 Put the strawberries, **JAM**, **MARGARINE** and **WATER** in the saucepan. Stir with the wooden spoon until mixed. Cook over medium heat for about 5 minutes, stirring all the time, until mixture is bubbly.

NUTRITION INFORMATION

2 TABLESPOONS: Calories 95 (Calories from Fat 20); Fat 2g (Saturated 1g); Cholesterol 0mg; Sodium 40mg; Carbohydrate 19g (Dietary Fiber 1g); Protein 0g

% DAILY VALUE: Vitamin A 2%; Vitamin C 8%; Calcium 0%; Iron 0%

DIET EXCHANGES: 1 Fruit; 1/2 Fat

Prep: Cook: Makes:

15 minutes 10 minutes 2 servings

Shake-'em-Up Scrambled Eggs

UTENSILS

Cutting board
Sharp knife
Medium-size jar with lid
Measuring cup
Measuring spoons
Medium skillet
Pancake turner
Toaster

INGREDIENTS

1 small tomato
2 eggs
1/4 cup shredded Cheddar cheese
1/8 teaspoon salt
2 teaspoons margarine or butter
2 slices bread

1 Wash the **TOMATO**. Chop tomato into small pieces on the cutting board, using the knife. Put tomato pieces in the clean jar.

2 Crack the **EGGS** on side of jar, letting eggs slip into jar. Add the **CHEESE** and **SALT** to tomato pieces and eggs. Cover jar tightly with the lid and shake well.

3 Put the **MARGARINE** in the skillet. Heat over medium heat until margarine is melted (you can tilt the skillet so inside of skillet will be coated with margarine).

4 Pour the egg mixture into skillet and cook without stirring. Stir eggs gently with the pancake turner when eggs in bottom of pan start to get firm. Cook 5 to 8 minutes longer or until eggs are slightly firm but not runny.

5 Toast the **BREAD** in the toaster. Cut each toast slice in half on the cutting board, using the knife. Serve scrambled eggs over toast slices.

NUTRITION INFORMATION

1 SERVING: Calories 240 (Calories from Fat 135); Fat 15g (Saturated 5g); Cholesterol 225mg; Sodium 490mg; Carbohydrate 15g (Dietary Fiber 1g); Protein 12g

% DAILY VALUE: Vitamin A 18%; Vitamin C 6%; Calcium 12%; Iron 8%

DIET EXCHANGES: 1 Starch, 1 Lean Meat, 2 Fat,

Mega-Chocolate Chip Muffins

UTENSILS

Muffin pan with medium cups
Small saucepan or microwavable
   bowl and waxed paper
Wooden spoon
Small mixing bowl
Measuring cups
Fork
Measuring spoons
Large mixing bowl
Toothpick
Pot holders
Wire cooling rack

INGREDIENTS

Cooking spray (or 12 paper
   baking cups)
1/2 cup (1 stick) margarine
   or butter
2 eggs
1 cup milk
2 cups all-purpose flour
3/4 cup packed brown sugar
1 tablespoon baking powder
1 teaspoon salt
1/2 cup semisweet chocolate chips

CHECK IT OUT!

Be on the lookout for UFOs. If you fill the muffin cups too full, the tops of your muffins may look more like flying saucers than breakfast treats!

1 Heat the oven to 400°. Spray each cup in muffin pan with the **COOKING SPRAY**, or put a paper baking cup in each muffin cup. Save for later (you will need the muffin pan in step 4).

2 Put the **MARGARINE** in the saucepan. Heat over low heat for about 1 minute, stirring a few times with the wooden spoon, until margarine is melted. Take saucepan off hot burner. (Or put margarine in the microwavable bowl. Cover bowl with waxed paper. Microwave on High 30 to 45 seconds or until margarine is melted.) Cool for 5 minutes.

3 Crack the **EGGS** on side of the small mixing bowl, letting eggs slip into bowl. Add melted margarine and **MILK** to eggs. Beat with the fork until well mixed.

4 Put the **FLOUR, BROWN SUGAR, BAKING POWDER** and **SALT** in the large mixing bowl. Stir with the wooden spoon until mixed. Add the milk mixture to flour mixture. Stir just until flour is wet (the batter should still be a little lumpy; you don't want it to be smooth). Stir in the **CHOCOLATE CHIPS**. Spoon batter into the sprayed muffin cups until cups are about 2/3 full.

5 Bake 18 to 20 minutes or until the muffins are golden brown and the toothpick poked in center of muffin comes out clean.

6 Use the pot holders to take muffin pan out of oven. Carefully tip pan on its side to take muffins out of cups, and put muffins on the wire cooling rack. Cool muffins on cooling rack 10 minutes before serving.

> Chocolate chips are what make these muffins soooo good and "chipalicious!"
> —SHARDAE

NUTRITION INFORMATION

1 MUFFIN: Calories 215 (Calories from Fat 65); Fat 7g (Saturated 2g); Cholesterol 35mg; Sodium 400mg; Carbohydrate 35g (Dietary Fiber 1g); Protein 4g

% DAILY VALUE: Vitamin A 6%; Vitamin C 0%; Calcium 10%; Iron 8%

DIET EXCHANGES: 2 Starch, 1 Fat

35

"Banana-O-Rama" Bread

INGREDIENTS

Cooking spray
3 medium bananas
1/2 cup (1 stick) margarine
   or butter
2 eggs
1 1/2 cups sugar
1/2 cup buttermilk
1 teaspoon vanilla
2 1/2 cups all-purpose flour
1 teaspoon baking soda
1 teaspoon salt

UTENSILS

Loaf pan, 9 x 5 inches
Large mixing bowl
Potato masher or fork
Small saucepan or microwavable
   bowl and waxed paper
Wooden spoon
Measuring cups
Measuring spoons
Toothpick
Pot holders
Table knife
Wire cooling rack

Here's another idea

Make **CHOCO-BANANA BREAD**: Stir 1/2 cup chocolate chips into the batter before you pour it into the pan.

1 Heat the oven to 350°. Spray just the bottom of the pan with the **COOKING SPRAY**. Save for later (you will need this in step 5).

2 Peel the **BANANAS**. Put bananas in the bowl. Mash bananas with the potato masher or fork until almost smooth.

3 Put the **MARGARINE** in the saucepan. Heat over low heat for about 1 minute, stirring a few times with the wooden spoon, until margarine is melted. Take saucepan off hot burner. (Or put margarine in the microwavable bowl. Cover bowl with waxed paper. Microwave on high 30 to 45 seconds or until margarine is melted.) Cool for 5 minutes.

4 Crack the **EGGS** on side of bowl, letting eggs slip into bowl. Add melted margarine, **SUGAR**, **BUTTERMILK** and **VANILLA** to bananas and eggs. Stir with the wooden spoon until mixed.

5 Add the **FLOUR, BAKING SODA** and **SALT** to sugar mixture. Stir just until flour is wet. Pour the batter into the sprayed pan.

6 Bake for about 1 hour and 15 minutes or until the toothpick poked in center of bread comes out clean. Use the pot holders to take pan out of oven. Cool bread in pan for 5 minutes.

7 Loosen the sides of bread from pan, using the knife. Carefully tip pan on its side and tap gently so that bread comes out of pan. Put bread on the wire cooling rack until no longer warm when touched.

I'd call this breakfast treat Disco Dancing Monkey Bread.
—**DRAKE**

NUTRITION INFORMATION

1 SLICE: Calories 225 (Calories from Fat 65); Fat 7g (Saturated 1g); Cholesterol 25mg; Sodium 320mg; Carbohydrate 39g (Dietary Fiber 1g); Protein 3g

% DAILY VALUE: Vitamin A 8%; Vitamin C 0%; Calcium 2%; Iron 6%

DIET EXCHANGES: 2 Starch, 1/2 Fruit, 1 Fat

Gooey Caramel Rolls

UTENSILS

Measuring cups
Round cake pan, 8 inches across
Spoon
Measuring spoons
Small mixing bowl
Sharp knife
Pot holders
Large heatproof plate

INGREDIENTS

1/2 cup packed dark brown sugar
1/3 cup whipping (heavy) cream
1/4 cup chopped pecans
2 tablespoons granulated sugar
1 teaspoon ground cinnamon
1 can (11 ounces) refrigerated soft
    breadsticks

this isn't my bed roll!

1. Heat the oven to 350°. Put the **BROWN SUGAR** and **WHIPPING CREAM** in the cake pan. Stir with the wooden spoon until mixed. Sprinkle with the **PECANS**. Save for later (you will need this in step 4).

2. Put the **GRANULATED SUGAR** and **CINNAMON** in the bowl! Stir with the spoon until mixed.

3. Open the can of **BREADSTICKS** and take out the dough. Unroll dough, but do not separate it into breadsticks. Sprinkle the cinnamon-sugar mixture over dough. Roll up dough, starting at one of the short ends.

4. Separate the dough at cut marks into spiral slices, using the knife. Put dough slices on top of the sauce in pan.

5. Bake for 25 minutes or until the rolls are golden brown. Use the pot holders to take pan out of oven. Cool for 1 minute. Turn pan upside down onto the plate to remove rolls. Leave pan over rolls for 1 minute so sauce will drizzle over rolls.

> When I made these rolls everyone wanted more. They're really "ooey" and gooey.
> **—NIKKI**

NUTRITION INFORMATION

1 ROLL: Calories 295 (Calories from Fat 80); Fat 9g (Saturated 3g); Cholesterol 15mg; Sodium 320mg; Carbohydrate 50g (Dietary Fiber 2g); Protein 5g

% DAILY VALUE: Vitamin A 2%; Vitamin C 0%; Calcium 6%; Iron 12%

DIET EXCHANGES: 2 Starch, 1 Fruit, 2 Fat

CHAPTER 2

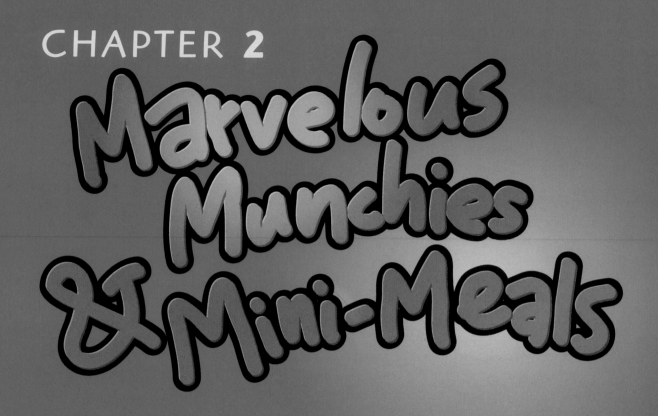

Where's it at?

Caramel C

UTeNSiLS

Measuring cups
Rectangular pan, 13 x 9 inches
Measuring spoons
Medium saucepan
Wooden spoon
Pot holders

iNGReDieNTS

6 cups popped popcorn (about
   1/4 cup unpopped)
1/2 cup packed brown sugar
1/4 cup (1/2 stick) margarine or butter
2 tablespoons light corn syrup
1/4 teaspoon salt
1/4 teaspoon baking soda

orn Commotion

1 Heat the oven to 200°. Put the **POPCORN** in the pan. Save for later (you will need this in step 4).

2 Put the **BROWN SUGAR, MARGARINE, CORN SYRUP** and **SALT** in the saucepan. Cook over medium heat, stirring a few times with the wooden spoon, until mixture is bubbly around edges. Keep cooking over medium heat for 5 minutes, stirring a few times.

3 Take the saucepan off hot burner. Stir in the **BAKING SODA** until mixture looks foamy.

4 Quickly pour the caramel mixture over popcorn in pan, and stir until popcorn is coated with caramel.

5 Bake for 1 hour, stirring every 15 minutes. Use the pot holders to take pan out of oven. Cool for 15 minutes before serving.

NUTRITION INFORMATION

1 CUP: Calories 200 (Calories from Fat 90); Fat 10g (Saturated 2g); Cholesterol 0mg; Sodium 330mg; Carbohydrate 27g (Dietary Fiber 1g); Protein 1g

% DAILY VALUE: Vitamin A 10%; Vitamin C 0%; Calcium 2%; Iron 2%

DIET EXCHANGES: 1 1/2 Starch, 2 Fat

43

15 minutes

7 cups

Good Ol' Gorp

iNGReDieNTS

4 cups Cheerios® cereal
1 cup raisins
1 cup salted peanuts
1/4 cup (1/2 stick) margarine
   or butter
1 bag (6 ounces) semisweet
   chocolate chips (1 cup)

UTeNSiLS

Measuring cups
Large mixing bowl
Spoon
Medium saucepan or microwavable
   bowl and waxed paper
Wooden spoon
Fork
Plastic bag with zipper top or plastic

44 container with lid

1 Put the **CEREAL**, **RAISINS** and **PEANUTS** in the bowl. Stir with the spoon until mixed.

2 Put the **MARGARINE** in the saucepan. Heat over low heat for about 1 minute, stirring a few times with the wooden spoon, until margarine is melted. Take saucepan off hot burner. (Or put margarine in the microwavable bowl. Cover bowl with waxed paper. Microwave on High 30 to 45 seconds or until margarine is melted.)

3 Pour the melted margarine over cereal mixture, using the fork to toss lightly until the mixture is coated.

4 Sprinkle the **CHOCOLATE CHIPS** over cereal mixture, then toss again.

5 Store the snack in the plastic bag or container.

NUTRITION INFORMATION

1/2 CUP: Calories 225 (Calories from Fat 115); Fat 13g (Saturated 4g); Cholesterol 0mg; Sodium 170mg; Carbohydrate 25g (Dietary Fiber 3g); Protein 5g

% DAILY VALUE: Vitamin A 14%; Vitamin C 8%; Calcium 4%; Iron 16%

DIET EXCHANGES: 1 1/2 Starch, 2 1/2 Fat

PRep: **Makes:**

15 minutes   **1** cup dip

UTeNSILS

Measuring cup
Measuring spoon
Small bowl
Spoon
Cutting board
Sharp knife
Toothpicks

iNGReDieNTS

1 cup vanilla yogurt
2 tablespoons packed brown sugar
Your favorite fruit (apple wedges, strawberries, banana slices, pineapple chunks, grapes)

Fantastic Fruit Dip

1 Put the **YOGURT** and **BROWN SUGAR** in the bowl. Stir with the spoon until mixed.

2 Cut the **FRUIT** on the cutting board, using the knife. Poke a toothpick into each piece of fruit. Dip the fruit into the yogurt mixture.

CHECK IT OUT!

For a funky, fun dip, add a few drops of your favorite food color to the yogurt and use granulated sugar instead of brown sugar. Toss in some candy sprinkles, and you'll really have an eye-popping, tongue-tempting fruit dip.

NUTRITION INFORMATION

2 TABLESPOONS DIP: Calories 40 (Calories from Fat 0); Fat 0g (Saturated 0g); Cholesterol 0mg; Sodium 20mg; Carbohydrate 9g (Dietary Fiber 0g); Protein 1g

% DAILY VALUE: Vitamin A 0%; Vitamin C 0%; Calcium 4%; Iron 0%

DIET EXCHANGES: 1/2 Fruit

10 minutes   **2** servings

Berry Bonanza Smoothie

UTENSILS

Measuring cups
Measuring spoons
Blender with lid
2 tall glasses
Straws

INGREDIENTS

1 container (8 ounces) strawberry
  or raspberry low-fat yogurt
1 cup milk
1 tablespoon powdered sugar
2 cups frozen (slightly thawed)
  whole strawberries

Here's another idea

Go ape! Make a **BERRY-BANANA BONANZA SMOOTHIE**: Peel a banana and cut it into chunks, using a knife. Toss the banana chunks in with the strawberries before blending.

1 Put the **YOGURT, MILK** and **POWDERED SUGAR** in the blender. Cover blender with lid, and blend on high speed about 30 seconds or until mixture is smooth.

2 Add half (1 cup) of the **STRAWBERRIES** to the yogurt mixture. Cover blender with lid, and blend on high speed for 1 minute. Add the rest of the strawberries. Cover blender with lid, and blend on high speed 1 minute longer or until mixture is smooth.

3 Pour the smoothie into the tall glasses. Serve right away with the straws.

This great, healthy treat tastes like a shake and is absolutely wonderful on a hot day.
—ALI

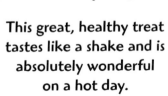

NUTRITION INFORMATION

1 SERVING: Calories 245 (Calories from Fat 35); Fat 4g (Saturated 2g); Cholesterol 15mg; Sodium 130mg; Carbohydrate 47g (Dietary Fiber 5g); Protein 10g

% DAILY VALUE: Vitamin A 8%; Vitamin C 100%; Calcium 34%; Iron 4%

DIET EXCHANGES: 2 Fruit, 1 Skim Milk, 1 Fat

PreP: Makes:

35 minutes

12 deviled eggs

Devilish Deviled Eggs

UteNSiLS

Medium saucepan with lid
Cutting board
Sharp knife
Spoon
Small mixing bowl
Fork
Measuring spoons

Blueberries

Ground Tumeric

Grape Juice

iNGReDieNTS

6 eggs
Cold water
3 tablespoons mayonnaise or
   salad dressing
1/2 teaspoon ground mustard (dry)
1/4 teaspoon salt
1/4 teaspoon pepper
Paprika, if you like

50

DYING TO DYE YOUR EGGS?

Make **EXCELLENT EASTER EGGS!** You can use a coloring kit from the supermarket, or try some of these natural dyes. You can find most of the ingredients in your kitchen cupboard or in the fridge.

HERE'S WHAT TO DO:

• Follow step 1 in the recipe, then pick a color from the chart (below), and add the ingredient to water in saucepan. If you like, add about 1 tablespoon of white vinegar to the water so the dye will stick better to the eggs.

• Follow step 2 in the recipe, then let the eggs cool in the saucepan. Takes eggs out of saucepan, and put them in a bowl. Store eggs in the refrigerator up to 24 hours.

1 Put the **EGGS** in the saucepan. Add enough **COLD WATER** to saucepan until water covers eggs.

COLOR	INGREDIENT
Yellow	Ground turmeric
Lavender	Fresh or frozen blueberries
Brown	Grape juice or strong brewed coffee

2 Heat the water and eggs to boiling over high heat. Take saucepan off the hot burner. Cover saucepan with lid, and put on the counter for 20 minutes.

3 Run cold water into the saucepan to quickly cool eggs and keep them from cooking more.

6 Mash the egg yolks with the fork until almost smooth. Add the **MAYONNAISE, MUSTARD, SALT** and **PEPPER**. Stir with the spoon until mixed.

4 Tap each egg lightly on the counter to crack the shell. Roll egg between your hands to loosen the shell, then peel it off. (If shell is hard to peel, you can hold the egg under cold water while peeling.)

7 Spoon the egg yolk mixture onto the egg whites. Sprinkle eggs with the **PAPRIKA**, if you like. Serve right away, or cover and put in the refrigerator up to 24 hours.

5 Cut each egg lengthwise in half on the cutting board, using the knife. Take the egg yolks out of the egg whites, using the spoon. Put the egg yolks in the bowl. Save the egg whites (you will need them in step 7).

NUTRITION INFORMATION

1 DEVILED EGG: Calories 55 (Calories from Fat 45); Fat 5g (Saturated 1g); Cholesterol 110mg; Sodium 150mg; Carbohydrate 0g (Dietary Fiber 0g); Protein 3g

% DAILY VALUE: Vitamin A 4%; Vitamin C 0%; Calcium 0%; Iron 2%

DIET EXCHANGES: 1 Medium-Fat Meat, 1/2 Fat

Prep: 15 minutes

Makes: 16 tortilla wheels

Tortilla Wheels

Ingredients

1 medium carrot
2/3 cup soft cream cheese with garden vegetables
2 flour tortillas (10 inches across)
6 slices thinly sliced cooked turkey
6 slices mozzarella cheese

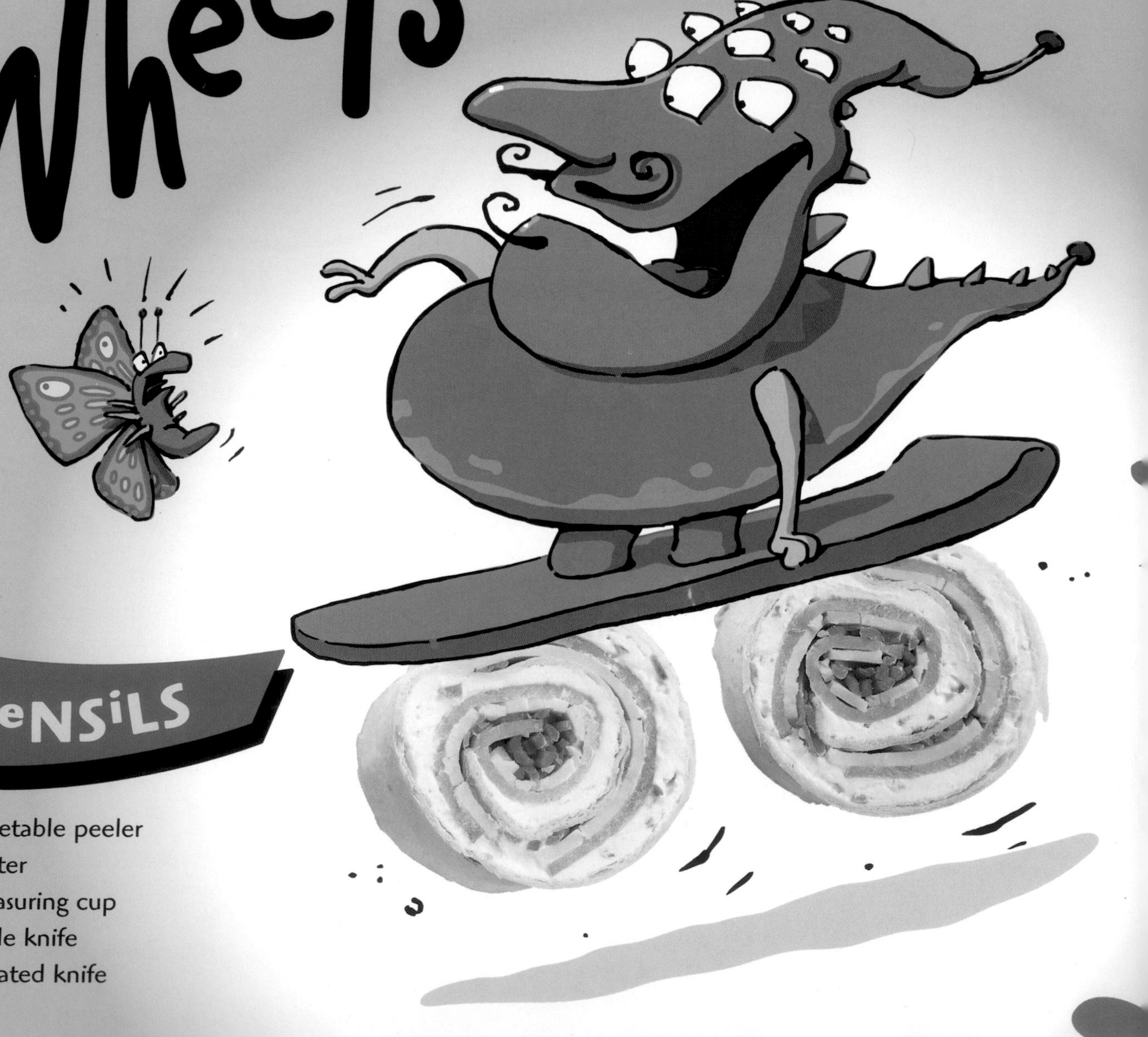

Utensils

Vegetable peeler
Grater
Measuring cup
Table knife
Serrated knife

CHECK IT OUT!

Chill — your rolls! Slicing the rolls into wheels is a breeze if you plan ahead and make them a few hours before you want to eat them. You can even wrap up the rolls in plastic wrap and put them in the refrigerator for up to 24 hours.

1 Peel the **CARROT** with the vegetable peeler.

2 Shred the carrot into long, skinny pieces, using the grater (you will need this in step 4).

3 Spread 1/3 cup of the **CREAM CHEESE** evenly over each **TORTILLA**, using the table knife.

4 Top each tortilla with 3 slices of the **TURKEY**, 3 slices of the **CHEESE** and half of the shredded carrots. Roll up the tortillas.

5 Cut each tortilla roll into 8 slices, using the serrated knife. Serve right away. Wrap any leftover slices with plastic wrap, and put them in the refrigerator.

NUTRITION INFORMATION

1 TORTILLA WHEEL: Calories 70 (Calories from Fat 35); Fat 4g (Saturated 2g); Cholesterol 10mg; Sodium 130mg; Carbohydrate 5g (Dietary Fiber 0g); Protein 3g

% DAILY VALUE: Vitamin A 8%; Vitamin C 0%; Calcium 6%; Iron 2%

DIET EXCHANGES: 1 Vegetable, 1 Fat

Puzzling Pretzels

UTENSILS

Measuring cups
Medium mixing bowl
Measuring spoons
Wooden spoon
Ruler, if you like
Cookie sheet
Small mixing bowl
Fork
Pastry brush
Pot holders
Pancake turner
Wire cooling rack

INGREDIENTS

1 1/2 cups all-purpose flour
2/3 cup milk
2 tablespoons vegetable oil
2 teaspoons baking powder
1 teaspoon sugar
1/2 teaspoon salt
2 tablespoons all-purpose flour
1 egg
Your favorite topping (coarse salt,
    cinnamon-sugar, oats or sesame
    seed), if you like

54

1 Heat the oven to 425°. Put the 1 1/2 cups **FLOUR, MILK, VEGETABLE OIL, BAKING POWDER, SUGAR** and **SALT** in the medium bowl. Stir with the wooden spoon to make a soft dough.

4 Crack the **EGG** on side of the small bowl, letting egg slip into bowl. Beat egg with the fork until yolk and white are mixed. Brush egg over pretzels, using the pastry brush. Sprinkle lightly with your favorite **TOPPING**, if you like.

2 Sprinkle the **2 TABLESPOONS FLOUR** over a clean surface, such as a kitchen counter or breadboard. Put dough on the surface. Divide dough in half to make 2 balls. Roll each ball of dough around 3 or 4 times. Curve your fingers around and fold dough toward you, then push it away with the heels of your hands, using a quick rocking motion. Repeat 10 times. Put bowl upside down over balls of dough for 15 minutes.

5 Bake 9 to 11 minutes or until the pretzels are light golden brown. Use the pot holders to take cookie sheet out of oven. Take pretzels off cookie sheet, using the pancake turner. Cool pretzels for 10 minutes on the wire cooling rack.

3 Divide each ball of dough into 8 pieces. Roll each piece into a 12-inch rope. Use the ruler to measure, if you like. Twist halves together to make a pretzel shape. Pinch ends to seal. Put pretzels on the cookie sheet (you do not need to grease the cookie sheet).

1   2

NUTRITION INFORMATION

1 PRETZEL: Calories 65 (Calories from Fat 20); Fat 2g (Saturated 0g); Cholesterol 15mg; Sodium 140mg; Carbohydrate 10g (Dietary Fiber 0g); Protein 2g

% DAILY VALUE: Vitamin A 0%; Vitamin C 0%; Calcium 4%; Iron 4%

DIET EXCHANGES: 1/2 Starch, 1/2 Fat

Mini-Pizza Poppers

UTENSILS

Measuring cups
Medium mixing bowl
Spoon
Round biscuit or cookie cutter,
   3 1/2 inches across
Cutting board
Small sharp knife
Pastry brush
Fork
Cookie sheet
Pot holders
Pancake turner
Wire cooling rack

KING of PIZZA

INGREDIENTS

1 package (15 ounces)
   refrigerated pie crusts
3 tablespoons pizza sauce
1/3 cup shredded
   mozzarella cheese
14 slices pepperoni
Extra pizza sauce, if you like

CHECK IT OUT!

Tuna cans rule! Even if you don't have a round biscuit or cookie cutter, you can still cut the pie crust into circles. Just put a clean tuna can (6-ounce size) on the pie crust, and press down to make a circle.

1 Heat the oven to 400°. Put the **PIE CRUSTS** on the counter for 15 minutes to soften.

2 Put the **PIZZA SAUCE** and **CHEESE** in the bowl. Stir with the spoon until mixed. Save for later (you will need this in step 5).

3 Unfold each pie crust. Take off the plastic sheets. Press out the fold lines on pie crusts, using your fingers. Cut each pie crust into seven 3 1/2-inch circles, using the biscuit or cookie cutter.

4 Cut each **PEPPERONI** slice in half on the cutting board, using the knife.

5 Put 2 pepperoni halves on center of each pie crust circle. Top with about 1 teaspoon of the cheese mixture.

6 Brush the edge of each pie crust circle with a little water, using the pastry brush. Fold each circle in half over filling. Press edges of circles with the fork to seal. Place pizza poppers on the cookie sheet (you do not need to grease the cookie sheet).

7 Bake 12 to 15 minutes or until the pizza poppers are light golden brown. Use the pot holders to take cookie sheet out of oven. Right away, take pizza poppers off cookie sheet, using the pancake turner. Cool for 5 minutes on the wire cooling rack before serving.

8 Serve the warm pizza poppers with the extra **PIZZA SAUCE** for dipping, if you like.

These pint-sized pepperoni pizza bites make a great party snack.
—ALY

NUTRITION INFORMATION

1 PIZZA POPPER: Calories 205 (Calories from Fat 125); Fat 14g (Saturated 4g); Cholesterol 8mg; Sodium 360mg; Carbohydrate 16g (Dietary Fiber 1g); Protein 5g

% DAILY VALUE: Vitamin A 0%; Vitamin C 0%; Calcium 4%; Iron 6%

DIET EXCHANGES: 1 Starch, 2 1/2 Fat

MUNCHIES

57

10 minutes **4** minutes **5** servings

Super Supreme Nachos

INGREDIENTS

25 tortilla chips
1/4 cup salsa
1 bag (4 ounces) shredded
   Cheddar cheese (1 cup)
Extra salsa, if you like

UTENSILS

Cookie sheet
Aluminum foil
Measuring cup
Spoon
Pot holders

CHECK IT OUT!

For a single-sized snack, you can zap these nachos in the microwave. Put 5 tortilla chips in a circle on a microwavable dinner plate. Spoon a small amount of salsa on each chip. Sprinkle with shredded cheese. Microwave uncovered on High 20 to 30 seconds or until cheese is melted.

1 Heat the oven to 400°. Cover the cookie sheet with the aluminum foil.

2 Put the **TORTILLA CHIPS** on foil-lined cookie sheet. Spoon the **SALSA** evenly over tortilla chips. Sprinkle the **CHEESE** on top of salsa and chips.

3 Bake for about 4 minutes or until the cheese is melted. Use the pot holders to take cookie sheet out of oven.

4 Serve the nachos with the **EXTRA SALSA**, if you like.

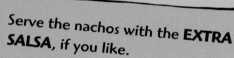

NUTRITION INFORMATION

1 SERVING: Calories 125 (Calories from Fat 80); Fat 9g (Saturated 5g); Cholesterol 20mg; Sodium 250mg; Carbohydrate 6g (Dietary Fiber 1g); Protein 6g

% DAILY VALUE: Vitamin A 8%; Vitamin C 4%; Calcium 16%; Iron 2%

DIET EXCHANGES: 1/2 Starch, 1/2 Medium-Fat Meat, 1 Fat

Outrageous Oven Fries

UTeNSiLS

Cookie sheet
Vegetable brush
Cutting board
Sharp knife
Ruler, if you like
Measuring spoon
Pancake turner
Pot holders

iNGReDieNTS

Cooking spray
2 large potatoes (about
    1 pound total)
2 tablespoons vegetable oil
Salt, if you like

1 Heat the oven to 450°. Spray the cookie sheet with the **COOKING SPRAY**.

2 Scrub the **POTATOES** with the vegetable brush. Cut each potato into 1/2-inch slices on the cutting board, using the knife. Use the ruler to measure, if you like. Cut slices into 1/2-inch strips. Put potato strips on the sprayed cookie sheet.

3 Drizzle the **VEGETABLE OIL** over the potatoes. Carefully toss potatoes with the pancake turner to coat them with oil.

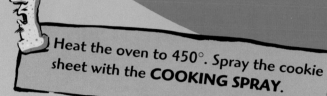

4 Bake for about 40 minutes, turning a few times with pancake turner, until the potatoes are golden brown. Use the pot holders to take cookie sheet out of oven.

5 Sprinkle the **SALT** over potatoes, if you like.

NUTRITION INFORMATION

1 SERVING: Calories 155 (Calories from Fat 65); Fat 7g (Saturated 1g); Cholesterol 0mg; Sodium 5mg; Carbohydrate 23g (Dietary Fiber 2g); Protein 2g

% DAILY VALUE: Vitamin A 0%; Vitamin C 10%; Calcium 0%; Iron 6%

DIET EXCHANGES: 1 1/2 Starch, 1 Fat

Prep: 15 minutes

Makes: 5 wraps

Confetti Ham & Cheese Wraps

UTENSILS

Measuring cups
Measuring spoons
Medium mixing bowl
Spoon
Toothpicks

INGREDIENTS

3/4 cup shredded Cheddar cheese
1/2 cup frozen (thawed) whole
   kernel corn (from a 10-ounce box)
2 tablespoons mayonnaise or
   salad dressing
2 tablespoons sour cream
5 flour tortillas (6 to 8 inches across)
5 slices fully cooked deli ham

CHECK IT OUT!

Wrap it and pack it! These wrap sandwiches make a great picnic lunch. Just make sure you put them in a cooler so they'll stay cold until you're ready to eat.

1 Put the **CHEESE, CORN, MAYONNAISE** and **SOUR CREAM** in the bowl. Stir with the spoon until mixed.

2 Top each **TORTILLA** with 1 slice of **HAM**. Spread 2 tablespoons of the corn mixture over each slice of ham, using the back of the spoon.

3 Roll up the tortillas. Poke a toothpick in center of each tortilla to keep it rolled up. Serve right away. Wrap any leftover sandwiches with plastic wrap, and put them in the refrigerator.

> Rice and beans and a dollop of guacamole make these wraps extra good.
> —NIKKI

NUTRITION INFORMATION

1 WRAP: Calories 235 (Calories from Fat 125); Fat 14g (Saturated 6g); Cholesterol 35mg; Sodium 505mg; Carbohydrate 17g (Dietary Fiber 1g); Protein 11g

% DAILY VALUE: Vitamin A 4%; Vitamin C 0%; Calcium 12%; Iron 6%

DIET EXCHANGES: 1 Starch, 1 Lean Meat, 2 Fat

Prep: **15** minutes

Makes: **4** sandwiches

"Tuna-trific" Sandwiches

UTeNSiLS

Can opener
Strainer
Medium mixing bowl
Measuring cup
Measuring spoons
Spoon
Table knife
Cookie cutters, if you like

It's Pisces!

iNGReDieNTS

1 can (9 ounces) tuna in water
1/2 cup mayonnaise or
   salad dressing
1 teaspoon lemon juice
1/4 teaspoon salt
1/4 teaspoon pepper
8 slices bread

64

> You don't have to smear this tuna spread on just bread. Anything goes—like buns, crackers or bagels.
>
> —JOE

1 Open the can of **TUNA** with the can opener. Put tuna in the strainer over the sink to drain. Put tuna in the bowl.

2 Add the **MAYONNAISE, LEMON JUICE, SALT** and **PEPPER** to tuna. Stir with the spoon until mixed.

3 Spread the tuna mixture evenly on 4 slices of the **BREAD**, using the knife. Top with the other 4 slices of bread.

4 Cut each sandwich in half, using the knife. Or cut the sandwiches into fun shapes, using the cookie cutters, if you like. Serve right away. Wrap any leftover sandwiches with plastic wrap, and put them in the refrigerator.

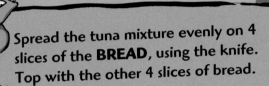

NUTRITION INFORMATION

1 SANDWICH: Calories 400 (Calories from Fat 215); Fat 24g (Saturated 4g); Cholesterol 35mg; Sodium 790mg; Carbohydrate 26g (Dietary Fiber 1g); Protein 21g

% DAILY VALUE: Vitamin A 2%; Vitamin C 0%; Calcium 6%; Iron 14%

DIET EXCHANGES: 2 Starch, 2 Lean Meat, 3 Fat

minutes   minutes   roll-ups

Hot Dog Roll-Ups

INGREDIENTS

1/4 cup (1/2 stick) margarine
   or butter
8 slices bread
2 teaspoons mustard
4 slices process American cheese
8 hot dogs
Mustard or ketchup, if you like

UTENSILS

Small saucepan or microwavable bowl
   and waxed paper
Wooden spoon
Cookie sheet
Pastry brush
Measuring spoon
Table knife
Sharp knife
Tongs
Toothpicks
Pot holders

1 Heat the oven to 375°. Put the **MARGARINE** in the saucepan. Heat over low heat for about 1 minute, stirring a few times with the wooden spoon, until margarine is melted. Take saucepan off hot burner. (Or put margarine in the microwavable bowl. Cover bowl with waxed paper. Microwave on High 30 to 45 seconds or until margarine is melted.)

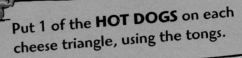

4 Put 1 of the **HOT DOGS** on each cheese triangle, using the tongs.

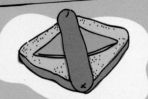

2 Put the **BREAD** slices on the cookie sheet. Brush about half of the melted margarine over bread slices, using the pastry brush. Spread with the **MUSTARD**, using the table knife.

5 Fold each slice of bread over hot dog and cheese to make a triangle shape. Fasten with 2 toothpicks, one on each side, by poking them through the bread and hot dog. Brush outsides of the bread triangles with the rest of the melted margarine.

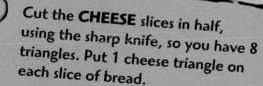

3 Cut the **CHEESE** slices in half, using the sharp knife, so you have 8 triangles. Put 1 cheese triangle on each slice of bread.

6 Bake 10 to 15 minutes or until the bread is golden brown. Use the pot holders to take cookie sheet out of oven.

7 Serve the roll-ups with the **MUSTARD** or **KETCHUP**, if you like.

NUTRITION INFORMATION

1 ROLL-UP: Calories 295 (Calories from Fat 205); Fat 23g (Saturated 8g); Cholesterol 35mg; Sodium 910mg; Carbohydrate 14g (Dietary Fiber 1g); Protein 9g

% DAILY VALUE: Vitamin A 10%; Vitamin C 0%; Calcium 8%; Iron 6%

DIET EXCHANGES: 1 Starch, 1 High-Fat Meat, 3 Fat

67

Double-Decker Grilled Cheese Sandwiches

Utensils

Table knife
Large skillet
Pancake turner

Ingredients

3 tablespoons margarine or
  butter, soft enough to spread
8 slices bread
4 slices Cheddar cheese
4 slices Monterey Jack or
  mozzarella cheese

Here's another idea

Make **SINGLE GRILLED CHEESE SANDWICHES:**
In step 2, top bread with 1 slice of your
favorite cheese.

1 Spread the **MARGARINE** evenly on 1 side of each **BREAD** slice, using the table knife.

2 Put 4 slices of bread with buttered sides down in the skillet. Top each with 1 slice of **CHEDDAR CHEESE** and 1 slice of **MONTEREY JACK CHEESE**. Top with the other 4 slices of bread, buttered sides up.

3 Cook uncovered over medium heat for about 5 minutes or until the bottoms of sandwiches are golden brown. Turn sandwiches over, using the pancake turner. Cook 2 to 3 minutes longer or until the bottoms are golden brown and cheese is melted.

NUTRITION INFORMATION

1 SANDWICH: Calories 380 (Calories from Fat 215); Fat 24g (Saturated 10g); Cholesterol 45mg; Sodium 650mg; Carbohydrate 27g (Dietary Fiber 1g); Protein 15g

% DAILY VALUE: Vitamin A 24%; Vitamin C 4%; Calcium 32%; Iron 10%

DIET EXCHANGES: 2 Starch, 1 Medium-Fat Meat, 3 Fat

CHAPTER 3

Dynamite Dinners & Other Big Stuff

ARF!

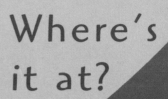

Where's it at?

Belt-Bustin' Burgers

INGREDIENTS

1 pound ground beef
1/4 teaspoon salt
1/8 teaspoon pepper
4 hamburger buns
Your favorite toppings (ketchup, mustard, tomatoes, lettuce, dill pickle slices)

UTENSILS

Measuring spoons
Medium mixing bowl
Fork
Ruler, if you like
Large skillet
Pancake turner
Small sharp knife
Cookie sheet, if you like
Pot holders

Here's another idea

Make **CHEESY CHEESEBURGERS**: After you flip the burgers, cook for about 4 minutes, then top each burger with 1 slice of cheese. Cook until cheese is melted.

1 Put the **GROUND BEEF, SALT** and **PEPPER** in the bowl. Stir with the fork until mixed.

2 Shape the beef mixture with your hands into 4 burgers. (They should be about 3/4 inch thick. Use the ruler to measure, if you like.)

3 Put the burgers in the skillet. Cook over medium heat for 5 minutes. Flip burgers over, using the pancake turner. Cook for about 5 minutes longer or until burgers are no longer pink in the middle. (To check if burgers are cooked, cut into the middle of a burger with the knife.)

4 Split each **HAMBURGER BUN** in half to make a top and a bottom. If you like, toast buns in oven (see note below). Put the burgers on the bottoms of the buns. Add your **FAVORITE TOPPINGS**. Cover with the tops of the buns.

NOTE:
To toast buns—Set the oven control to broil. Put bun halves, cut side up, on a cookie sheet. Put cookie sheet in oven so tops of the buns are 4 to 5 inches from heat. Toast buns about 1 minute or until buns are light brown. Watch carefully! Use the pot holders to take cookie sheet out of oven.

NUTRITION INFORMATION

1 BURGER: Calories 345 (Calories from Fat 160); Fat 18g (Saturated 7g); Cholesterol 65mg; Sodium 440mg; Carbohydrate 22g (Dietary Fiber 1g); Protein 25g

% DAILY VALUE: Vitamin A 0%; Vitamin C 0%; Calcium 6%; Iron 18%

DIET EXCHANGES: 1 1/2 Starch, 3 Medium-Fat Meat

Gloppy Sloppy Joes

UTeNSiLS

Paper towels
Cutting board
Sharp knife
Large skillet
Long-handled spoon
Strainer
Small bowl
Measuring spoon

iNGReDieNTS

1 medium onion, if you like
1 medium stalk celery
1 pound ground beef
1/8 teaspoon pepper
1 jar (16 ounces) spaghetti sauce
6 hamburger buns

1 If you use the **ONION**, peel the outside layer of skin from it. Wash onion and the **CELERY** in cool water. Pat dry with the paper towels. Chop onion and celery into small pieces on the cutting board, using the knife. Save for later (you will need them in step 4).

4 Add the chopped onion, chopped celery, **PEPPER** and **SPAGHETTI SAUCE** to beef. Heat to boiling, stirring all the time. Turn the heat down to low. Cook for 10 minutes, stirring a few times.

2 Put the **GROUND BEEF** in the skillet. Stir with the long-handled spoon until beef is broken into small pieces. Cook over medium heat 8 to 10 minutes, stirring often, until beef is brown.

5 Split each **HAMBURGER BUN** in half to make a top and a bottom. Spoon sloppy joe mixture onto the bottoms of the buns. Cover with the tops of the buns.

3 Take the skillet off hot burner. Put the strainer over the small bowl. Spoon beef into strainer to drain the fat. Put beef back in skillet.

NUTRITION INFORMATION

1 SLOPPY JOE: Calories 360 (Calories from Fat 145); Fat 16g (Saturated 5g); Cholesterol 45mg; Sodium 650mg; Carbohydrate 38g (Dietary Fiber 3g); Protein 19g

% DAILY VALUE: Vitamin A 6%; Vitamin C 10%; Calcium 8%; Iron 18%

DIET EXCHANGES: 2 Starch, 1 Medium-Fat Meat, 2 Vegetable, 2 Fat

15 minutes **15** minutes **10** tacos

Totally Terrific Tacos

UTENSILS

Paper towels
Cutting board
Sharp knife
3 small serving bowls
Large skillet
Long-handled spoon
Strainer
Small bowl
Measuring cup
Large serving bowl
Tongs, for serving
Serving spoons, for serving

TA DA!

INGREDIENTS

1/2 head lettuce
1 tomato
1 bag (4 ounces) shredded
   Cheddar cheese (1 cup)
1 pound ground beef
1 cup salsa
10 taco shells

Here's another idea

Make a **TACO SALAD**: Put the lettuce in a large bowl or on a large serving platter. Top with the chopped tomato, cheese, cooked ground beef and salsa. Sprinkle with 2 cups crushed tortilla chips.

1 Wash the **LETTUCE** in cool water. Pat dry with the paper towels. Cut lettuce into long pieces on the cutting board, using the knife. Put lettuce in one of the small serving bowls.

6 Add the **SALSA** to beef. Heat to boiling, stirring all the time. Turn the heat down to medium-low. Cook 5 minutes, stirring a few times. Pour beef mixture into the large serving bowl.

2 Wash the **TOMATO** in cool water. Pat dry with paper towels. Chop the tomato into small pieces on cutting board, using knife. Put tomato pieces in another small serving bowl.

7 Heat the **TACO SHELLS** as directed on package, if you like. Serve taco shells with the beef mixture, lettuce, tomato and cheese, letting each person make his or her own taco.

3 Put the **CHEESE** in the third small serving bowl.

4 Put the **GROUND BEEF** in the skillet. Stir with the long-handled spoon until beef is broken into small pieces. Cook over medium heat 8 to 10 minutes, stirring often, until beef is brown.

CHECK IT OUT!

Want a veggie version? Open a 16-ounce can of refried beans, and dump them into a saucepan. Cook over medium heat about 5 minutes, stirring a few times with a wooden spoon, until beans are warm. Spoon beans into a serving bowl, and serve with the salsa and the other taco toppings.

5 Take the skillet off hot burner. Put the strainer over the small bowl. Spoon beef into strainer to drain the fat. Put beef back in skillet.

NUTRITION INFORMATION

1 TACO: Calories 205 (Calories from Fat 115); Fat 13g (Saturated 5g); Cholesterol 40mg; Sodium 210mg; Carbohydrate 11g (Dietary Fiber 2g); Protein 13g

% DAILY VALUE: Vitamin A 6%; Vitamin C 6%; Calcium 10%; Iron 8%

DIET EXCHANGES: 1 1/2 Starch, 1 1/2 Medium-Fat Meat, 1 Vegetable, 1 Fat

Chill-Chasin' Chili

iNGReDieNTS

1 pound ground beef
1 can (14 1/2 ounces) diced tomatoes
1 tablespoon chili powder
1/2 teaspoon garlic salt
1/8 teaspoon red pepper sauce
1 can (15 to 16 ounces) red
kidney beans
1/4 cup shredded Cheddar cheese

UTeNSiLS

Large saucepan
Long-handled spoon
Strainer
Small bowl
Can opener
Measuring spoons
Measuring cup

1 Put the **GROUND BEEF** in the saucepan. Stir with the long-handled spoon until beef is broken into small pieces. Cook over medium heat 8 to 10 minutes, stirring often, until beef is brown.

2 Take saucepan off hot burner. Put the strainer over the small bowl. Spoon beef into strainer to drain the fat. Put beef back in saucepan.

3 Open the can of **TOMATOES** with the can opener. Add the tomatoes (with the liquid in the can), **CHILI POWDER, GARLIC SALT** and **RED PEPPER SAUCE** to beef. Stir until mixed. Heat to boiling over medium-high heat, stirring a few times. Turn the heat down to low. Cook for 30 minutes, stirring a few times.

4 Open the can of **KIDNEY BEANS** with the can opener. Add the beans (with the liquid in the can) to beef mixture. Stir until mixed. Cook for 20 minutes longer.

5 Take saucepan off hot burner. Top each serving of chili with the **CHEESE**.

NUTRITION INFORMATION

1 SERVING: Calories 390 (Calories from Fat 160); Fat 18g (Saturated 7g); Cholesterol 70mg; Sodium 630mg; Carbohydrate 33g (Dietary Fiber 9g); Protein 33g

% DAILY VALUE: Vitamin A 12%; Vitamin C 16%; Calcium 10%; Iron 32%

DIET EXCHANGES: 2 Starch, 3 1/2 Lean Meat, 1 Vegetable

CAUTION HOT SAUCE

Meatballs & Twisters

Utensils

- Paper towels
- Cutting board
- Sharp knife
- Medium mixing bowl
- Fork
- Large skillet
- Long-handled spoon
- Large saucepan with lid
- Measuring cup
- Wooden spoon
- Colander

HOME PLATE

Ingredients

- 1 small onion, if you like
- 1 slice bread
- 3/4 pound ground beef
- Cooking spray
- 1 jar (26 ounces) spaghetti sauce (3 cups)
- Water
- 3 cups uncooked rotelle (spiral) pasta or your favorite pasta

CHECK IT OUT!

Turning plain pasta into a kaleidoscope of colors is as easy to do as it is colorful! For 2 cups of water, add 15 to 20 drops of food color. Then heat the water and cook the pasta as it says in the recipe. If you want a mix of colors, use two separate saucepans and choose a color for each. Or you can cook and drain one batch of colored pasta, then use the same saucepan to make the next color.

1 If you use the **ONION**, peel the outside layer of skin from it. Wash onion in cool water. Pat dry with the paper towels. Chop onion into small pieces on the cutting board, using the knife.

2 Tear the **BREAD** into very small pieces. Put bread pieces in the bowl.

3 Add the **GROUND BEEF** and chopped onion to bread. Stir with the fork until mixed. Shape the mixture with your hands into small meatballs. (The meatballs should be about the size of large marbles.)

4 Spray the skillet with the **COOKING SPRAY**. Heat over medium-high heat. Put meatballs in skillet. Cook, turning with the long-handled spoon, until they are brown on all sides.

5 Add the **SPAGHETTI SAUCE** to meatballs. Stir with the long-handled spoon until mixed. Cook for about 15 minutes or until meatballs are no longer pink in the center. (To check if meatballs are cooked, cut one open with a clean knife.)

6 While the sauce is cooking, fill the saucepan with **WATER** until about half full. Cover saucepan with lid, and heat over medium-high heat until water is boiling fast. Add the **PASTA** to water. Heat to boiling again. Boil uncovered 10 to 12 minutes, stirring often with the wooden spoon, until pasta is soft but not mushy.

7 Pour the pasta into the colander over the sink to drain. Serve pasta with meatballs and sauce.

> I dished up this delicious dish and served it to my sister with a tall glass of cold milk. It's definitely sister approved!
>
> **—LAUREN**

NUTRITION INFORMATION

1 SERVING: Calories 480 (Calories from Fat 135); Fat 14g (Saturated 4g); Cholesterol 30mg; Sodium 660mg; Carbohydrate 70g (Dietary Fiber 4g); Protein 20g

% DAILY VALUE: Vitamin A 10%; Vitamin C 14%; Calcium 4%; Iron 22%

DIET EXCHANGES: 4 Starch, 1/2 Medium-Fat Meat, 2 Vegetables, 2 Fat

Zoned-Out Calzones

UTENSILS

Large skillet
Long-handled spoon
Strainer
Small bowl
Measuring cups
Measuring spoons
Large mixing bowl
Wooden spoon

Rolling pin
Ruler, if you like
2 cookie sheets
Fork
Pot holders
Pancake turner
Wire cooling rack
Sharp knife

INGREDIENTS

1 pound ground beef
3/4 cup pizza sauce
5 cups Bisquick Original baking mix
3/4 cup water
3 tablespoons vegetable oil
2 tablespoons Bisquick Original
   baking mix
1 1/3 cups shredded Cheddar cheese

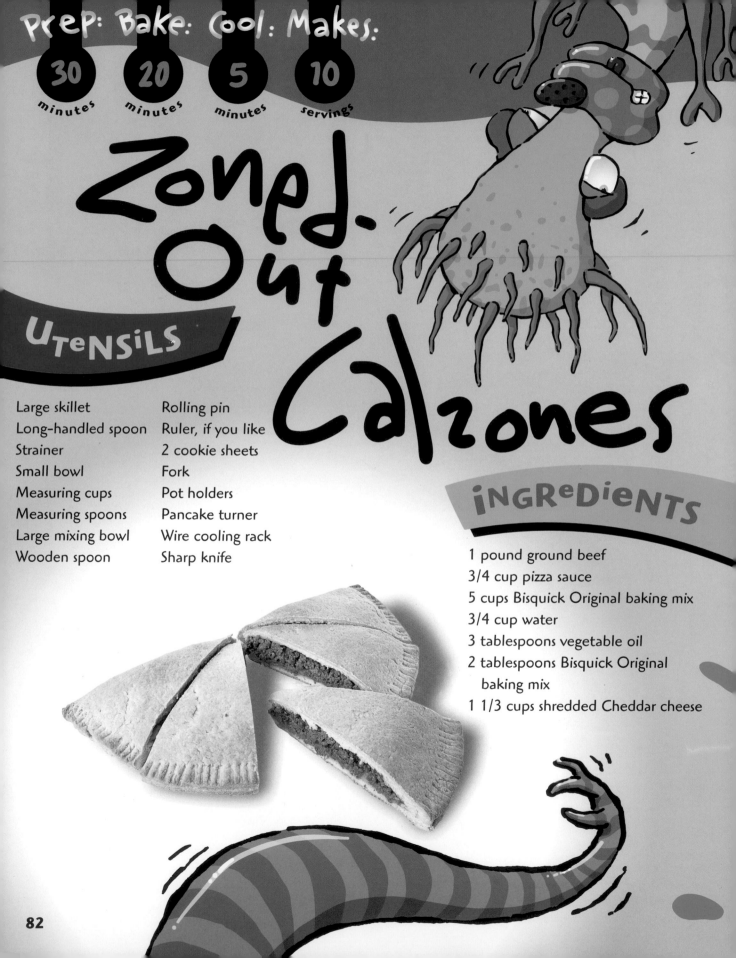

82

CHECK IT OUT!

If you can't fit two cookie sheets side by side in your oven, bake one calzone while you make the second one.

1 Heat the oven to 450°. Put the **GROUND BEEF** in the skillet. Stir with the long-handled spoon until beef is broken into small pieces. Cook over medium heat 8 to 10 minutes, stirring often, until beef is brown.

2 Take the skillet off hot burner. Put the strainer over the small bowl. Spoon beef into strainer to drain the fat. Put beef back in skillet.

3 Add the **PIZZA SAUCE** to beef. Stir with the long-handled spoon until mixed. Save beef mixture for later (you will need this in step 5).

4 Put the 5 cups **BAKING MIX, WATER** and **VEGETABLE OIL** in the large bowl. Stir with the wooden spoon to make a dough (dough will be dry). Sprinkle the 2 tablespoons **BAKING MIX** over a clean surface, such as a kitchen counter or breadboard. Put dough on the surface. Gently roll dough in baking mix to coat all sides. Shape dough into a ball. Curve your fingers around and fold dough toward you, then push it away with the heels of your hands, using a quick rocking motion. Repeat 5 times or until dough is smooth.

5 Divide the dough in half. Roll each half into a 12-inch circle, using the rolling pin. Use the ruler to measure, if you like. Place 1 dough circle on each cookie sheet (you do not need to grease the cookie sheets). Top half of each circle with the **CHEESE**. Top cheese with the beef mixture. Fold the other half of each circle over filling. Press the edges together with the fork to seal.

1   2

6 Bake 15 to 20 minutes or until the calzones are golden brown. Use the pot holders to take cookie sheet out of oven. Right away, take calzones off cookie sheet using the pancake turner. Cool for 5 minutes on the wire cooling rack. Cut each calzone into 5 wedges, using the knife.

NUTRITION INFORMATION

1 SERVING: Calories 440 (Calories from Fat 225); Fat 25g (Saturated 9g); Cholesterol 40mg; Sodium 1030mg; Carbohydrate 38g (Dietary Fiber 1g); Protein 16g

% DAILY VALUE: Vitamin A 4%; Vitamin C 4%; Calcium 18%; Iron 16%

DIET EXCHANGES: 2 1/2 Starch, 1 High-Fat Meat, 3 Fat

UTeNSiLS

Round pizza pan, 12 inches across, or
    rectangular pan, 13 x 9 inches
Pastry brush
Pot holders
Wire cooling rack
Measuring cups
Rubber scraper
Cutting board
Sharp knife
Pizza cutter

Whatever Pizza

iNGReDieNTS

Shortening (to grease pan)
1 can (10 ounces) refrigerated
    pizza dough
1 cup pizza sauce
Toppings:
  • 1/2 cup chopped green bell
    pepper
  • 1/4 cup sliced ripe olives
  • 1/2 package (3 1/2-ounce size)
    thinly sliced pepperoni
  • 1/4 pound hamburger or
    sausage, cooked

1 bag (6 ounces) shredded
mozzarella cheese (1 1/2 cups)

1 Heat the oven to 425°. Grease the pizza pan or rectangular pan with the **SHORTENING**, using the pastry brush.

2 Open the can of **PIZZA DOUGH**, and take out the dough. Unroll dough and press into the greased pan, using your hands.

3 Bake for about 10 minutes or until the crust is light golden brown. Use the pot holders to take pan out of oven. Cool for 5 minutes on the wire cooling rack.

4 Spread the **PIZZA SAUCE** evenly over dough, using the rubber scraper.

5 Choose 2 or 3 **TOPPINGS**, and sprinkle them over the sauce. Sprinkle the **CHEESE** over toppings.

6 Use the pot holders to put pan back in oven. Bake 12 to 15 minutes or until crust is golden brown and cheese is melted. Use pot holders to take pan out of oven. Cool for 5 minutes on wire cooling rack. Cut pizza into wedges, using the pizza cutter.

NUTRITION INFORMATION

1 SERVING: Calories 320 (Calories from Fat 145); Fat 16g (Saturated 6g); Cholesterol 30mg; Sodium 740mg; Carbohydrate 29g (Dietary Fiber 2g); Protein 19g

% DAILY VALUE: Vitamin A 8%; Vitamin C 18%; Calcium 22%; Iron 14%

DIET EXCHANGES: 2 Starch, 1 1/2 Medium-Fat Meat, 1 Fat

20 minutes **50** minutes **6** servings

Kickin' Oven-Fried Chicken

UTENSILS

Rectangular pan, 13 x 9 inches

Wooden spoon

Small saucepan or microwavable bowl
  and waxed paper

Pastry brush with sliding bristle holder

Measuring cup

Measuring spoons

Plastic bag with zipper top

Tongs

Pot holders

Small sharp knife

INGREDIENTS

Cooking spray

2 tablespoons margarine or butter

3- to 3 1/2-pound cut-up broiler-
  fryer chicken

2/3 cup Bisquick Original baking mix

1 1/2 teaspoons paprika

1/4 teaspoon salt

1/4 teaspoon pepper

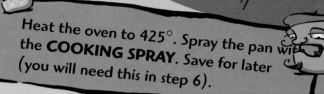

1 Heat the oven to 425°. Spray the pan with the **COOKING SPRAY**. Save for later (you will need this in step 6).

5 Drop the chicken, 1 piece at a time, into bag. Seal bag closed. Shake bag to coat chicken with mixture. Throw away any leftover mixture in bag.

2 Put the **MARGARINE** in the saucepan. Heat over low heat, stirring a few times with the wooden spoon, until margarine is melted. Take saucepan off hot burner. (Or put margarine in the microwavable bowl. Cover bowl with waxed paper. Microwave on High 15 to 20 seconds or until margarine is melted.)

6 Put the chicken pieces, skin sides down, in the sprayed pan. Bake for 35 minutes. Turn chicken pieces over, using the tongs. Bake for about 15 minutes longer or until juice of chicken is no longer pink when centers of thickest pieces are cut. (To check if chicken is cooked, use the pot holders to take pan out of oven, then cut into the thickest piece of chicken with the knife.)

3 Brush the **CHICKEN** with some of the melted margerine, using the pastry brush.

4 Put the rest of the margarine, **BAKING MIX**, **PAPRIKA**, **SALT** and **PEPPER** in the plastic bag. Seal bag closed. Shake bag until ingredients are mixed.

NUTRITION INFORMATION

1 SERVING: Calories 295 (Calories from Fat 155); Fat 17g (Saturated 5g); Cholesterol 85mg; Sodium 390mg; Carbohydrate 8g (Dietary Fiber 0g); Protein 28g

% DAILY VALUE: Vitamin A 10%; Vitamin C 0%; Calcium 4%; Iron 10%

DIET EXCHANGES: 1 1/2 Starch, 4 Lean Meat, 1 Fat

Crunchy Chicken Tenders

INGREDIENTS

Cooking spray
3/4 cup cornflakes cereal
1/2 cup all-purpose flour
3/4 teaspoon salt
1/2 teaspoon pepper
1/3 cup buttermilk or milk
1 pound chicken breast tenders

UTENSILS

Rectangular pan, 13 x 9 inches
Aluminum foil
Measuring cups
Measuring spoons
Plastic bag with zipper top
Rolling pin
Medium mixing bowl
Pot holders
Small sharp knife

SNAP

CHECK IT OUT!

Can't find chicken breast tenders at your supermarket? No problem! Use 1 pound boneless, skinless chicken breast halves instead. Just cut each chicken breast half into 6 strips on a plastic cutting board, using a sharp knife.

1 Heat the oven to 400°. Line the pan with the aluminum foil. Spray foil with the **COOKING SPRAY**. Save for later (you will need this in step 4).

4 Put the coated chicken on lined and sprayed pan. Spray chicken with cooking spray.

2 Put the **CEREAL, FLOUR, SALT** and **PEPPER** in the plastic bag. Seal bag closed. Use the rolling pin to crush cereal.

5 Bake 25 to 30 minutes or until the coating is crisp and chicken is no longer pink in center. (To check if chicken is cooked, use the pot holders to take pan out of oven, then cut into the thickest piece of chicken with the knife.)

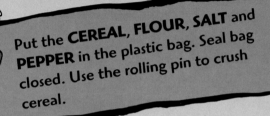

3 Pour the **BUTTERMILK** into the bowl. Dip the **CHICKEN** into buttermilk. Drop buttermilk-coated chicken, a few pieces at a time, into cereal mixture. Seal bag closed. Shake bag to coat chicken with cereal mixture. Throw away any leftover mixture in bag.

NUTRITION INFORMATION

1 SERVING: Calories 270 (Calories from Fat 55); Fat 6g (Saturated 2g); Cholesterol 100mg; Sodium 600mg; Carbohydrate 17g (Dietary Fiber 1g); Protein 38g

% DAILY VALUE: Vitamin A 4%; Vitamin C 2%; Calcium 4%; Iron 20%

DIET EXCHANGES: 1 Starch, 5 Very Lean Meat

Prep: 15 minutes | Cook: 10 minutes | Makes: 4 servings

Sizzling Chicken Stir-Fry

Utensils

- Measuring cups
- Large saucepan with lid
- Wooden spoon
- Pot holder
- Plastic cutting board
- Small sharp knife
- Measuring spoon
- Large skillet
- Pancake turner

Ingredients

- 1 cup water
- 1 cup uncooked instant rice
- 4 boneless, skinless chicken breasts (about 1 pound total)
- 1 tablespoon vegetable oil
- 1 bag (16 ounces) frozen broccoli, carrots and water chestnuts (or other combination)
- 1/3 cup stir-fry sauce

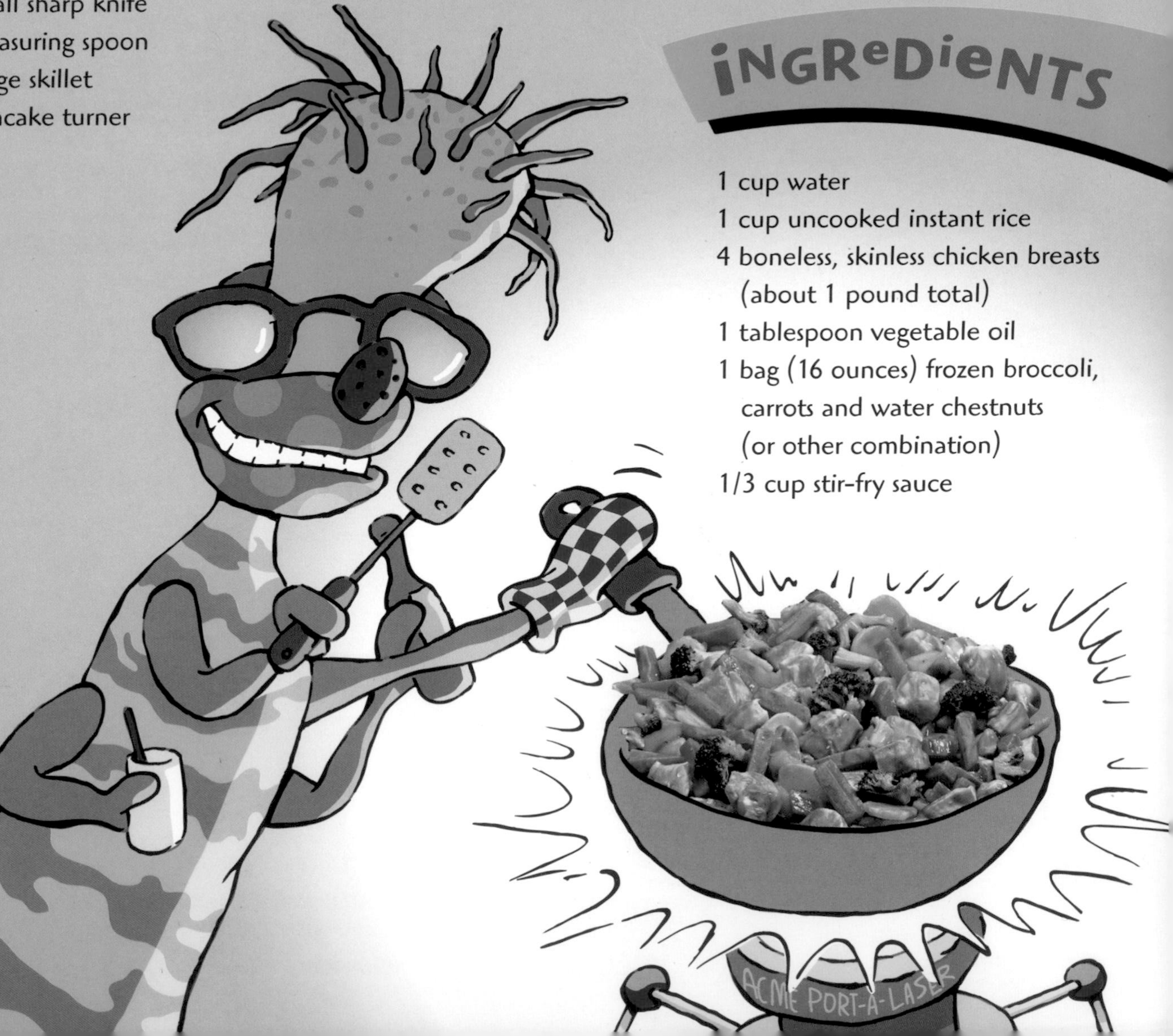
ACME PORT-A-LASER

1 Put the **WATER** in the saucepan. Cover saucepan with lid, and heat over medium-high heat until water is boiling fast. Take saucepan off hot burner.

2 Add the **RICE** to water, stirring with the wooden spoon. Cover saucepan with lid. Put saucepan on the pot holder on the counter while you cook the chicken.

3 Cut the **CHICKEN** into bite-size pieces on the cutting board, using the knife.

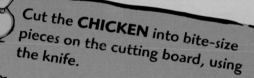

4 Put the **VEGETABLE OIL** in the skillet. Heat over medium-high heat until hot. (To test skillet, sprinkle with a few drops of water. If bubbles jump around, heat is just right.) Add the chicken. Cook for 2 minutes, stirring all the time with the pancake turner.

5 Add the **FROZEN VEGETABLES** to chicken. Cook for about 5 minutes, stirring all the time, until vegetables are slightly soft and chicken is no longer pink in center. (To check if chicken is cooked, cut into a piece with a clean knife.)

6 Add the **STIR-FRY SAUCE** to chicken mixture. Cook and stir for about 1 minute or until sauce is hot. Serve over the hot rice.

Veggies with Chicken Specs, that's what I'd call this recipe!
— BECKY

NUTRITION INFORMATION

1 SERVING: Calories 330 (Calories from Fat 70); Fat 8g; (Saturated 2g); Cholesterol 75mg; Sodium 1020mg; Carbohydrate 36g (Dietary Fiber 3g); Protein 32g

% DAILY VALUE: Vitamin A 94%; Vitamin C 38%; Calcium 4%; Iron 16%

DIET EXCHANGES: 2 Starch, 1 Vegetable, 3 1/2 Very Lean Meat, 1 Fat

Chicken Caboodle Noodle Soup

INGREDIENTS

2 cans (14 1/2 ounces each)
   ready-to-serve chicken broth
2 cups uncooked egg noodles
   or other pasta
2 sprigs fresh parsley
1 cup cut-up cooked chicken
Crackers, if you like

UTENSILS

Can opener
Large saucepan with lid
Measuring cups
Wooden spoon
Paper towels
Kitchen scissors

1 Open the cans of **CHICKEN BROTH** with the can opener. Pour broth into the saucepan. Cover saucepan with lid, and heat over medium-high heat until broth is boiling fast.

2 Add the **NOODLES** to broth. Heat to boiling again. Boil uncovered 6 to 8 minutes, stirring a few times with the wooden spoon, until noodles are soft but not mushy.

3 While the soup is cooking, rinse the **PARSLEY** in cool water. Pat dry with the paper towels. Cut parsley into small pieces, using the scissors.

4 Take the saucepan off hot burner. Stir parsley and the **CHICKEN** into soup. Serve with the **CRACKERS**, if you like.

NUTRITION INFORMATION

1 SERVING: Calories 175 (Calories from Fat 45); Fat 5g (Saturated 1g); Cholesterol 50mg; Sodium 980mg; Carbohydrate 15g (Dietary Fiber 0g); Protein 15g

% DAILY VALUE: Vitamin A 0%; Vitamin C 0%; Calcium 2%; Iron 10%

DIET EXCHANGES: 1 Starch, 2 Lean Meat

INGREDIENTS

10 flour tortillas (6 to 8 inches across)
2 tablespoons vegetable oil
1 bag (8 ounces) shredded
   Monterey Jack cheese (2 cups)
1 cup chopped cooked chicken
Salsa, if you like

Flying Saucer Chicken Quesadillas

It's a Family reunion!

UTENSILS

Measuring spoon
Pastry brush
Cutting board
Measuring cup
Large skillet
Pancake turner
Pizza cutter or kitchen scissors

CHECK IT OUT!

Looking for the easy way out? Build the quesadillas on a cookie sheet, and bake them in a 350° oven for 5 to 7 minutes.

1 Brush 1 side of each **TORTILLA** with some of the **VEGETABLE OIL**, using the pastry brush. Put 5 of the tortillas on the cutting board, oil sides down.

2 Sprinkle the **CHEESE** evenly over the 5 tortillas. Sprinkle the **CHICKEN** evenly over the cheese. Top with the rest of the tortillas, oil sides up.

3 Put 1 quesadilla in the skillet. Cook over medium-high heat for 2 minutes. Flip the quesadilla over, using the pancake turner. Cook for about 2 minutes longer or until bottom tortilla is light golden brown and cheese is melted. Take quesadilla out of skillet, using pancake turner. Repeat with the rest of the quesadillas.

4 Cut each quesadilla into 6 triangles on the cutting board, using the pizza cutter or kitchen scissors. Serve with the **SALSA**, if you like.

> Try turkey instead of chicken and top it all off with sour cream and salsa—yum!
>
> **—JOE**

NUTRITION INFORMATION

1 SERVING: Calories 400 (Calories from Fat 205); Fat 23g (Saturated 10g); Cholesterol 65mg; Sodium 540mg; Carbohydrate 27g (Dietary Fiber 2g); Protein 23g

% DAILY VALUE: Vitamin A 14%; Vitamin C 0%; Calcium 38%; Iron 12%

DIET EXCHANGES: 2 Starch, 2 1/2 High-Fat Meat

Double-Dipper Fish-Stick Fondue

Seein' I'm Double!

UTENSILS

Cutting board
Sharp knife
2 small bowls
Measuring cups
Measuring spoons
Spoon
Cookie sheet
Pot holders
Pancake turner
Serving platter
Toothpicks

INGREDIENTS

2 boxes (8 ounces each) frozen
  breaded fish sticks
1 large dill pickle
1/2 cup mayonnaise or salad
  dressing
1 teaspoon prepared horseradish
1/2 teaspoon onion powder
1/2 cup chili sauce
1 teaspoon lemon juice
1/4 teaspoon Worcestershire sauce
Pretzel sticks, if you like

1 Heat the oven as directed on the box of fish sticks. Put the **FISH STICKS** on the counter for 10 minutes.

5 Cut each fish stick into 3 pieces on cutting board, using knife. Put fish pieces on the cookie sheet.

2 Chop the **DILL PICKLE** into small pieces on the cutting board, using the knife. Put pickle pieces in one of the bowls.

6 Bake the fish pieces as directed on the box. Use the pot holders to take cookie sheet out of oven. Put fish pieces on the serving platter, using the pancake turner.

3 Add the **MAYONNAISE, HORSERADISH** and **ONION POWDER** to pickle pieces. Stir with the spoon until mixed.

7 To serve, poke a toothpick into each piece of fish. Or if you like, use **PRETZEL STICKS** instead of toothpicks. Dunk fish into the dips.

4 Put the **CHILI SAUCE, LEMON JUICE** and **WORCESTERSHIRE SAUCE** in the other bowl. Stir with the spoon until mixed.

NUTRITION INFORMATION

1 SERVING: Calories 355 (Calories from Fat 225); Fat 25g (Saturated 4g); Cholesterol 30mg; Sodium 920mg; Carbohydrate 23g (Dietary Fiber 1g); Protein 10g

% DAILY VALUE: Vitamin A 4%; Vitamin C 2%; Calcium 12%; Iron 6%

DIET EXCHANGES: 1 1/2 Starch, 1 Medium-Fat Meat, 4 Fat

97

Lazy-Day Lasagna

UTENSILS

Measuring spoons
Medium bowl
Spoon
Measuring cups
Rectangular baking dish,
   13 x 9 inches
Pot holders
Sharp knife

INGREDIENTS

1 container (15 ounces) ricotta cheese

2 tablespoons grated Parmesan cheese

1 teaspoon Italian seasoning

1 jar (26 ounces) spaghetti sauce (3 cups)

8 uncooked lasagna noodles

1 bag (8 ounces) shredded mozzarella cheese (2 cups)

1 Heat the oven to 350°. Put the **RICOTTA CHEESE, PARMESAN CHEESE** and **ITALIAN SEASONING** in the bowl. Stir with the spoon until mixed.

5 Bake 40 to 45 minutes or until the lasagna is hot in center and cheese is melted. Use the pot holders to take pan out of oven—it will be very hot and heavy. Let lasagna cool for 15 minutes. Cut into 4 rows by 2 rows, using the knife.

2 Spoon 1 cup of the **SPAGHETTI SAUCE** evenly over bottom of the baking dish. Top with 4 of the uncooked **LASAGNA NOODLES**.

3 Spread 1 cup of the ricotta cheese mixture over noodles, using the back of the spoon. Sprinkle with 1 cup of the **MOZZARELLA CHEESE**.

4 Spread 1 cup of the spaghetti sauce over mozzarella cheese. Make more layers with 4 lasagna noodles, the rest of the ricotta cheese mixture and 1 cup spaghetti sauce. (Be sure the spaghetti sauce completely covers the noodles.) Sprinkle with the rest of the mozzarella cheese.

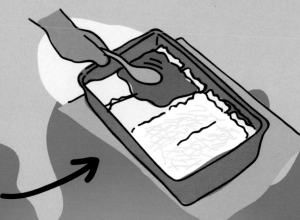

NUTRITION INFORMATION

1 SERVING: Calories 330 (Calories from Fat 115); Fat 13g (Saturated 6g); Cholesterol 30mg; Sodium 700mg; Carbohydrate 37g (Dietary Fiber 2g); Protein 18g

% DAILY VALUE: Vitamin A 16%; Vitamin C 10%; Calcium 40%; Iron 10%

DIET EXCHANGES: 2 Starch, 1 Lean Meat, 1 Vegetable, 2 Fat

99

UTENSILS

2 large saucepans with lids
Measuring cups
Wooden spoon
Measuring spoons
Colander

INGREDIENTS

Water
2 cups uncooked elbow macaroni
1/4 cup (1/2 stick) margarine
  or butter
1/4 cup all-purpose flour
1/2 teaspoon salt
1/4 teaspoon pepper
2 cups milk
1 bag (8 ounces) shredded
  Cheddar cheese (2 cups) or 8
  slices process American cheese

Marvelous Mac 'n' Cheese

CHECK IT OUT!

Macaroni mania! You can use elbow, shell or cork-screw macaroni in this recipe—the choice is yours.

1 Fill one of the saucepans with **WATER** until it is about half full. Cover saucepan with lid, and heat over medium-high heat until water is boiling fast.

5 Take the saucepan with flour mixture off hot burner. Slowly stir in the **MILK**. Put saucepan back on burner. Heat to boiling, stirring all the time. Boil and stir for 1 minute.

2 Add the **MACARONI** to water. Heat to boiling again. Boil uncovered 8 to 10 minutes, stirring often with the wooden spoon, until macaroni is soft but not mushy.

6 Add the **CHEESE** to sauce mixture. Stir with wooden spoon until cheese is melted.

3 While the macaroni is cooking, put the **MARGARINE** in the other saucepan. Heat over low heat for about 1 minute, stirring a few times with the wooden spoon, until margarine is melted.

7 Pour the macaroni into the colander over the sink to drain. Add macaroni to cheese mixture. Stir with wooden spoon until mixed.

4 Add the **FLOUR**, **SALT** and **PEPPER** to melted margarine. Stir with wooden spoon until mixed.

NUTRITION INFORMATION

1 SERVING: Calories 415 (Calories from Fat 200); Fat 22g (Saturated 10g); Cholesterol 45mg; Sodium 570mg; Carbohydrate 38g (Dietary Fiber 2g); Protein 18g

% DAILY VALUE: Vitamin A 22%; Vitamin C 0%; Calcium 30%; Iron 10%

DIET EXCHANGES: 2 Starch, 1 Milk, 1 High-Fat Meat, 2 1/2 Fat

Prep: Cook: Makes:

20 minutes **5** minutes **6** burritos

Lean, Mean, Bean Burritos

INGREDIENTS

12 sprigs cilantro, if you like
1 can (8 ounces) refried beans
6 flour tortillas (6 to 8 inches across)
3/4 cup shredded Monterey Jack cheese
Taco sauce or salsa, if you like

UTENSILS

Paper towels
Kitchen scissors
Can opener
Small saucepan
Wooden spoon
Measuring spoon
Table knife
Measuring cup
Sharp knife

GRRR...

CHECK IT OUT!

Cilantro looks very much like parsley and is often called Mexican or Chinese parsley. It has a cool, slightly sweet flavor that really tastes great with Mexican foods. You can use both the stems and leaves.

1 If you use the **CILANTRO**, rinse it in cool water. Pat dry with the paper towels. Cut cilantro into tiny pieces, using the scissors. Save for later (you will need this in step 4).

2 Open the can of **REFRIED BEANS** with the can opener. Put the beans in the saucepan. Cook over medium heat for about 5 minutes, stirring a few times with the wooden spoon, until beans are warm.

3 Spread about 3 tablespoons of the beans over each **TORTILLA**, using the table knife, until beans are almost to the edges of the tortillas.

4 Sprinkle the **CHEESE** evenly over each tortilla. Sprinkle chopped cilantro over cheese.

5 Fold 1 end of each tortilla up about 1 inch over filling. Fold the right and left sides over the folded end so the sides overlap. Fold the remaining end over.

1   2   3

6 Cut each burrito in half, using the sharp knife. Serve with the **TACO SAUCE** or **SALSA**, if you like.

NUTRITION INFORMATION

1 BURRITO: Calories 415 (Calories from Fat 205); Fat 23g (Saturated 8g); Cholesterol 35mg; Sodium 1000mg; Carbohydrate 38g (Dietary Fiber 1g); Protein 15g

% DAILY VALUE: Vitamin A 4%; Vitamin C 2%; Calcium 16%; Iron 14%

DIET EXCHANGES: 2 Starch, 1 Medium-Fat Meat, 1 Vegetable, 3 Fat

Mash 'em, Smash 'em Potatoes

INGREDIENTS

- 6 medium potatoes (about 2 pounds total)
- 2 1/2 cups water
- 1/2 cup milk
- 1/4 cup (1/2 stick) margarine or butter, soft enough to spread
- 1/2 teaspoon salt
- 1/8 teaspoon pepper

KA-CHUNK

UTENSILS

Vegetable brush
Vegetable peeler
Cutting board
Sharp knife
Measuring cups
Large saucepan with lid
Fork
Colander
Potato masher
Measuring spoons

1 Scrub the **POTATOES** with the vegetable brush. Peel skins from potatoes, using the vegetable peeler.

5 Take the saucepan off hot burner. Dump potatoes into the colander over the sink to drain. Put potatoes back in saucepan. Shake saucepan gently over low heat until water has disappeared.

2 Cut the potatoes into large pieces on the cutting board, using the knife.

6 Mash the potatoes with the potato masher until smooth and no lumps are left. Add the **MILK**, a little at a time, and mash some more.

7 Add the **MARGARINE**, **SALT** and **PEPPER** to potatoes. Mash until mixed.

3 Pour the **WATER** into the saucepan. Cover saucepan with lid, and heat over medium-high heat until water is boiling fast.

4 Add the potatoes to water. Cover saucepan with lid, and heat to boiling. When water is boiling, turn the heat down just enough so water bubbles gently. Cover saucepan with lid, and cook 20 to 25 minutes or until potatoes are soft when poked with the fork.

NUTRITION INFORMATION

1 SERVING: Calories 170 (Calories from Fat 70); Fat 8g (Saturated 2g); Cholesterol 2mg; Sodium 310mg; Carbohydrate 22g (Dietary Fiber 1g); Protein 3g

% DAILY VALUE: Vitamin A 12%; Vitamin C 10%; Calcium 2%; Iron 2%

DIET EXCHANGES: 1 Starch, 1 Vegetable, 1 1/2 Fat

DESSERTS

Where's it at?

iNGReDiENTS

1 egg

1 pouch (10.25 ounces)
fudge brownie mix (2 1/4 cups)

3 tablespoons vegetable oil

3 tablespoons water

1 box (4-serving size) chocolate
fudge pudding and pie filling
mix (not instant)

2 cups very hot water

Chocolate or vanilla ice cream,
if you like

UTeNSiLS

Small casserole dish (1 1/2-quart size)
Measuring spoons
Wooden spoon
Measuring cup
Medium mixing bowl
Pot holders
Serving bowls

Puddle-Of-Fudge Cake

1 Heat the oven to 400°. Crack the **EGG** on side of the casserole dish, letting egg slip into dish. Add the dry **BROWNIE MIX**, **VEGETABLE OIL** and 3 tablespoons **WATER** to egg. Stir with the wooden spoon until well mixed.

2 Put the dry **PUDDING MIX** and very **HOT WATER** in the medium bowl. Stir with wooden spoon until mixed. Carefully pour pudding mixture over brownie batter in dish.

3 Bake 35 to 40 minutes or until the pudding bubbles around edge of dish. Use the pot holders to take dish out of oven.

4 Serve the warm fudge cake in serving bowls with a scoop of the **ICE CREAM**, if you like.

NUTRITION INFORMATION

1 SERVING: Calories 325 (Calories from Fat 100); Fat 11g (Saturated 2g); Cholesterol 35mg; Sodium 210mg; Carbohydrate 53g (Dietary Fiber 0g); Protein 3g

% DAILY VALUE: Vitamin A 0%; Vitamin C 0%; Calcium 2%; Iron 4%

DIET EXCHANGES: Not recommended

Dalmation Cupcakes

INGREDIENTS

Cooking spray (or 24 paper baking cups)

3 eggs

1 box (1 pound 2.25 ounces) white cake mix with pudding

1 1/4 cups water

1/3 cup vegetable oil

1 cup miniature semisweet chocolate chips

1 tub (16 ounces) vanilla ready-to-spread frosting

Extra miniature semisweet chocolate chips

UTENSILS

Muffin pan with medium cups

Large mixing bowl

Measuring cups

Electric mixer

Rubber scraper

Wooden spoon

Toothpick

Pot holders

Wire cooling rack

Table knife or small metal spatula

1. Heat the oven to 350°. Spray each cup in muffin pan with the **COOKING SPRAY**, or put a paper baking cup in each muffin cup. Save for later (you will need this in step 3).

2. Crack the **EGGS** on side of the bowl, letting eggs slip into bowl. Add the dry **CAKE MIX**, **WATER** and **VEGETABLE OIL** to eggs. Beat with the electric mixer on low speed for 1 minute. Turn off mixer. Scrape side of bowl with the rubber scraper, then beat on low speed for 1 minute longer.

3. Add the 1 cup **CHOCOLATE CHIPS**. Stir with the wooden spoon until mixed. Spoon batter into the sprayed muffin cups until cups are about 2/3 full.

4. Bake 15 to 20 minutes or until the toothpick poked in center of cupcake comes out clean. Use the pot holders to take muffin pan out of oven. Cool the cupcakes for 10 minutes in muffin pan. Carefully tip pan on its side to take cupcakes out of cups, and put cupcakes on the wire cooling rack. Cool cupcakes before frosting them.

5. Spread the **FROSTING** over the cupcakes, using the table knife or spatula. Sprinkle the extra **CHOCOLATE CHIPS** on top of each cupcake.

CHECK IT OUT!

If you want the cupcakes to be as white as snow, use 3 egg whites instead of the whole eggs.

When you put the chocolate chips in the batter, sneak some for yourself. Mmm!

—CHRIS

NUTRITION INFORMATION

1 CUPCAKE: Calories 240 (Calories from Fat 90); Fat 10g (Saturated 5g); Cholesterol 25mg; Sodium 160mg; Carbohydrate 36g (Dietary Fiber 0g); Protein 2g

% DAILY VALUE: Vitamin A 0%; Vitamin C 0%; Calcium 2%; Iron 4%

DIET EXCHANGES: 2 Starch, 2 Fat

40 minutes **15** minutes **6** servings

Very Berry Shortcakes

Utensils

Measuring cups
Colander
Paper towels
Cutting board
Small sharp knife
Medium mixing bowl
Spoon
Plastic wrap
Measuring spoons
Large mixing bowl
Wooden spoon
Rolling pin
Ruler, if you like
Round cookie cutter,
    3 inches across
Cookie sheet
Pot holders
Pancake turner
Wire cooling rack
Dessert plates

Ingredients

Strawberries
1 quart (4 cups) whole
    strawberries
1/2 cup sugar

Shortcakes
2 1/3 cups Bisquick Original
    baking mix
1/2 cup half-and-half
3 tablespoons sugar
3 tablespoons margarine or
    butter, soft enough to spread
2 tablespoons Bisquick Original
    baking mix
1 cup frozen (thawed) whipped
    topping

WHO ARE YOU CALLIN' SHORT, BUSTER?

112

CHECK IT OUT!

If you don't have any of the frozen stuff, whip up a batch of real whipped cream. Here's how—put 1/2 cup whipping (heavy) cream and 2 tablespoons sugar in a chilled bowl. Beat with an electric mixer on high speed until cream makes stiff peaks when you pull the beaters out of it.

1 Put the **STRAWBERRIES** in the colander. Rinse with cool water. Gently pat strawberries dry with the paper towels.

2 Remove the stems from strawberries. Cut strawberries into bite-size pieces on the cutting board, using the knife. Put strawberries in the medium bowl.

3 Add the 1/2 cup **SUGAR** to strawberries. Gently stir with the wooden spoon. Cover bowl with the plastic wrap, and put in refrigerator.

4 Heat the oven to 425°. Make the **Shortcakes** by putting the 2 1/3 cups **BAKING MIX, HALF-AND-HALF**, 3 tablespoons **SUGAR** and **MARGARINE** in the large bowl. Stir with wooden spoon to make a soft dough.

5 Sprinkle the 2 tablespoons **BAKING MIX** over a clean surface (such as a kitchen counter or breadboard). Put dough on surface. Roll ball of dough around 3 or 4 times. Curve your fingers around and fold dough toward you, then push it away with the heels of your hands, using a quick rocking motion. Repeat 10 times.

6 Roll the dough with the rolling pin or pat the dough with your hands until 1/2 inch thick. Use the ruler to measure, if you like. Dip the cookie cutter into a small amount of baking mix, then cut the dough with the cookie cutter. Carefully put dough on the cookie sheet (you do not need to grease the cookie sheet).

7 Bake 12 to 15 minutes or until the shortcakes are golden brown. Use the pot holders to take cookie sheet out of oven. Take shortcakes off cookie sheet, using the pancake turner. Cool shortcakes on the wire cooling rack before topping them.

8 Cut the shortcakes in half to make a top and a bottom. Put bottom of shortcakes on the dessert plates. Spoon some of the strawberries over the shortcake bottoms. Cover with shortcake tops. Top with the rest of the strawberries and the **WHIPPED TOPPING**.

NUTRITION INFORMATION

1 SERVING: Calories 445 (Calories from Fat 190); Fat 21g (Saturated 8g); Cholesterol 30mg; Sodium 760mg; Carbohydrate 62g (Dietary Fiber 3g); Protein 5g

% DAILY VALUE: Vitamin A 14%; Vitamin C 44%; Calcium 12%; Iron 10%

DIET EXCHANGES: Not recommended

113

INGREDIENTS

4 medium cooking apples (such as Rome Beauty, Granny Smith or Greening)
1/4 cup firmly packed brown sugar
1/2 teaspoon ground cinnamon
1/4 cup water
1 cup all-purpose flour
2/3 cup granulated sugar
1/2 cup (1 stick) margarine or butter, soft enough to spread
Ice cream, if you like

UTENSILS

Cutting board
Small sharp knife
Measuring cups
Square pan, 8 x 8 inches
Measuring spoons
Small mixing bowl
Spoon
Medium mixing bowl
Pot holders
Wire cooling rack

"Apple-Ca-Dapple" Crisp

CHECK IT OUT!

Apples have real peel appeal. You don't have to peel the apples—if you leave the peel on, just make sure you take out the core and seeds.

1 Heat the oven to 375°. Cut each of the **APPLES** into 4 sections on the cutting board, using the knife. Cut out the apple core and seeds. Peel apple sections with the knife.

4 Put the **FLOUR, GRANULATED SUGAR** and **MARGARINE** in the medium bowl. Mix with your hands until the mixture is crumbly. Sprinkle crumbly mixture over apples.

2 Cut the apple sections into slices (you should have about 4 cups). Put apple slices in the pan.

3 Put the **BROWN SUGAR** and **CINNAMON** in the small bowl. Stir with the spoon until mixed. Sprinkle sugar mixture over apples. Pour the **WATER** over apples.

5 Bake 45 to 50 minutes or until the apples are soft and topping is golden brown. Use the pot holders to take pan out of oven. Cool for 10 minutes on the wire cooling rack.

6 Serve with the **ICE CREAM**, if you like.

NUTRITION INFORMATION

1 SERVING: Calories 420 (Calories from Fat 145); Fat 16g (Saturated 3g); Cholesterol 0mg; Sodium 210mg; Carbohydrate 70g (Dietary Fiber 3g); Protein 2g

% DAILY VALUE: Vitamin A 20%; Vitamin C 4%; Calcium 2%; Iron 8%

DIET EXCHANGES: Not recommended

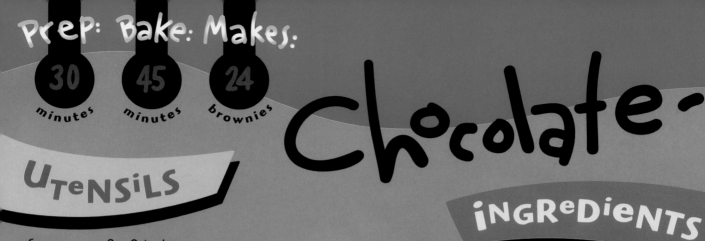

Prep: 30 minutes **Bake:** 45 minutes **Makes:** 24 brownies

Chocolate·

Utensils

Square pan, 9 x 9 inches
Pastry brush
Medium saucepan
Wooden spoon
Large mixing bowl
Measuring cups
Measuring spoons
Electric mixer
Pot holders
Wire cooling rack
Table knife or small spatula

Ingredients

Brownies

Shortening (to grease pan)
5 ounces unsweetened
   baking chocolate
2/3 cup margarine or butter
3 eggs
1 3/4 cups granulated sugar
2 teaspoons vanilla
1 cup all-purpose flour
1 bag (6 ounces) semisweet
   chocolate chips (1 cup)
1 cup chopped nuts, if you like

Chocolate Frosting

2 ounces unsweetened
   baking chocolate
2 tablespoons margarine or
   butter
2 cups powdered sugar
3 tablespoons hot water

116

Overload Brownies

1 Heat the oven to 350°. Grease the pan with the **SHORTENING**, using the pastry brush. Save for later (you will need this in step 5).

2 Put the 5 ounces **CHOCOLATE** and 2/3 cup **MARGARINE** in the saucepan. Heat over low heat, stirring a few times with the wooden spoon, until chocolate is melted. Take saucepan off hot burner. Cool for 5 minutes.

3 Crack the **EGGS** on side of the bowl, letting eggs slip into bowl. Add the **GRANULATED SUGAR** and **VANILLA** to eggs. Beat with the electric mixer on high speed for 5 minutes.

4 Add the melted chocolate mixture to sugar mixture. Beat with electric mixer on low speed for 2 minutes. Add the **FLOUR** to chocolate mixture. Stir with the wooden spoon until mixed.

5 Stir in the **CHOCOLATE CHIPS** and, if you like, the **NUTS**. Spread the batter in the greased pan, using the back of the spoon.

6 Bake 40 to 45 minutes or just until the brownies begin to pull away from sides of pan. Use the pot holders to take pan out of oven. Put pan on the wire cooling rack. Cool brownies before frosting them.

7 While the brownies are cooling, make the **Chocolate Frosting** by putting the 2 ounces **CHOCOLATE** and 2 tablespoons **MARGARINE** in saucepan. Heat over low heat, stirring a few times with the wooden spoon, until chocolate is melted. Take saucepan off hot burner.

8 Add the **POWDERED SUGAR** and **HOT WATER** to chocolate mixture. Stir until smooth.

9 Spread the frosting over the brownies, using the table knife or spatula. Cut pan of brownies into 6 rows by 4 rows using the knife.

NUTRITION INFORMATION

1 BROWNIE: Calories 255 (Calories from Fat 120); Fat 13g (Saturated 5g); Cholesterol 25mg; Sodium 90mg; Carbohydrate 35g (Dietary Fiber 2g); Protein 3g

% DAILY VALUE: Vitamin A 8%; Vitamin C 0%; Calcium 0%; Iron 6%

DIET EXCHANGES: 2 Starch, 2 Fat

25 minutes   **25** minutes   **48** bars

Rainbow Glitter Bars

UTeNSiLS

Jelly roll pan, 15 x 10 inches
Pastry Brush
Egg separator
Small mixing bowl
Large mixing bowl
Measuring cups
Wooden spoon
Measuring spoons
Plastic bag with zipper top
Eggbeater or wire whisk
Pot holders
Sharp knife
Wire cooling rack

"All that Glitters is not Dessert"

iNGReDieNTS

Bars
Shortening (to grease pan)
1 egg
1 cup granulated sugar
1 cup (2 sticks) margarine or
   butter, soft enough to spread
2 cups all-purpose flour
1/2 teaspoon ground cinnamon

Glitter Sugar
1/2 cup granulated sugar
Food colors (on top of
   page 119)
1 tablespoon water

GLITTER SUGAR COLORS

Color	Number of Drops of Liquid Food Color
Orange	2 drops yellow and 2 drops red
Yellow	4 drops yellow
Green	8 drops green
Blue	5 drops blue
Turquoise blue	3 drops blue and 1 drop green
Purple	3 drops red and 2 drops blue
Red	10 drops red

1 Heat the oven to 350°. Grease the pan with the **SHORTENING**, using the pastry brush. Save for later (you will need this in step 4).

2 Put the egg separator over the small bowl. Crack the **EGG** on side of the bowl. Open shell, letting yolk fall into center of separator. Let egg white slip through slots of separator into bowl. Save the egg white (you will need it in step 6).

3 Put the egg yolk, 1 cup **GRANULATED SUGAR** and **MARGARINE** in the large bowl. Stir with the wooden spoon until mixed.

4 Add the **FLOUR** and **CINNAMON** to sugar mixture. Stir until mixed. Press dough in the greased pan, using your hands.

5 Make one or more colors of Glitter Sugar by putting the 1/2 cup **GRANULATED SUGAR** in the plastic bag. Pick a color from the chart above, and add the **FOOD COLORS** to sugar. Seal bag closed. Squeeze the sugar in the bag until it becomes colored.

6 Add the **WATER** to the egg white in small bowl. Beat with the eggbeater or wire whisk until mixture looks foamy. Brush egg white mixture over dough, using the pastry brush. Sprinkle Glitter Sugar lightly over dough. (If you want to make a rainbow design, make semicircles of each color.)

7 Bake 20 to 25 minutes or until the bars are very light brown. Use the pot holders to take pan out of oven. Right away, cut pan of bars into 8 rows by 6 rows, using the sharp knife. Put pan on the wire cooling rack. Cool bars until they are no longer warm when touched.

Be creative with the sugar colors and make a picture on these yummy bars.

—DANNA

NUTRITION INFORMATION

1 BAR: Calories 85 (Calories from Fat 45); Fat 5g (Saturated 1g); Cholesterol 5mg; Sodium 60mg; Carbohydrate 9g (Dietary Fiber 0g); Protein 1g

% DAILY VALUE: Vitamin A 6%; Vitamin C 0%; Calcium 0%; Iron 2%

DIET EXCHANGES: 1/2 Starch, 1 Fat

Outrageous Candy Cookies

UTeNSiLS

Large mixing bowl
Measuring cups
Wooden spoon
Measuring spoons
Cookie sheet
Pot holders
Pancake turner
Wire cooling rack

iNGReDieNTS

1 egg
1/2 cup granulated sugar
1/2 cup packed brown sugar
1/2 cup (1 stick) margarine or
    butter, soft enough to spread
1 1/2 cups all-purpose flour
1/2 teaspoon baking soda
1/2 teaspoon salt
1 cup candy-coated
    chocolate candies

Here's another idea

Make **COOKIE POPS**: In step 3, poke a wooden stick (the kind with rounded ends) into the side of each drop of dough until the end of the stick is in the middle. Then follow directions for step 4.

1 Heat the oven to 375°. Crack the **EGG** on side of the bowl, letting egg slip into bowl. Add the **GRANULATED SUGAR**, **BROWN SUGAR** and **MARGARINE** to egg. Stir with the wooden spoon until mixed.

2 Add the **FLOUR, BAKING SODA** and **SALT** to sugar mixture. Stir until mixed.

3 Stir the **CANDIES** into the dough. Drop dough by rounded tablespoonfuls onto the cookie sheet (you do not need to grease the cookie sheet).

Here's another idea

Make **OUTRAGEOUS CHOCOLATE CHIP COOKIES**: Use 1 cup semisweet chocolate chips instead of the candy-coated chocolate candies.

4 Bake 10 to 12 minutes or until the cookies are light brown. Use the pot holders to take cookie sheet out of oven. Cool cookies on cookie sheet for 1 minute. Take cookies off cookie sheet, using the pancake turner, and put them on the wire cooling rack to finish cooling.

NUTRITION INFORMATION

1 COOKIE: Calories 140 (Calories from Fat 55); Fat 6g (Saturated 2g); Cholesterol 10mg; Sodium 135mg; Carbohydrate 21g (Dietary Fiber 0g); Protein 1g

% DAILY VALUE: Vitamin A 6%; Vitamin C 0%; Calcium 2%; Iron 2%

DIET EXCHANGES: 1 Starch, 1 Fat

Prep:	Bake:	Cool:	Makes:
20 minutes	**10** minutes each batch	**2** minutes	**36** cookies

Peanutty Butter Cookies

iNGReDieNTS

1 egg
1/2 cup granulated sugar
1/2 cup packed brown sugar
1/2 cup peanut butter
1/4 cup shortening
1/4 cup (1/2 stick) margarine or
  butter, soft enough to spread
1 1/4 cups all-purpose or whole
  wheat flour
3/4 teaspoon baking soda
1/2 teaspoon baking powder
1/4 teaspoon salt

UTeNSiLS

Large mixing bowl
Measuring cups
Wooden spoon
Measuring spoons
Ruler, if you like
Cookie sheet
Fork
Pot holders
Pancake turner
Wire cooling rack

Here's another idea

Make **ICE-CREAM SANDWICHES**: Put 1 rounded tablespoon ice cream on the bottom of a baked Peanutty Butter Cookie. Top with another cookie, then press cookies together. If you like, roll the edges of sandwiches in small candies or chopped peanuts. Wrap each sandwich in plastic wrap, and put in the freezer for about 1 hour or until firm.

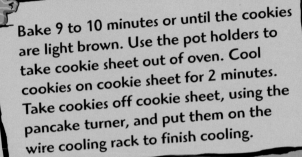

1 Heat the oven to 375°. Crack the **EGG** on side of the bowl, letting the egg slip into the bowl. Add the **GRANULATED SUGAR, BROWN SUGAR, PEANUT BUTTER, SHORTENING** and **MARGARINE** to egg. Stir with the wooden spoon until mixed.

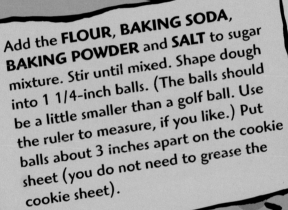

2 Add the **FLOUR, BAKING SODA, BAKING POWDER** and **SALT** to sugar mixture. Stir until mixed. Shape dough into 1 1/4-inch balls. (The balls should be a little smaller than a golf ball. Use the ruler to measure, if you like.) Put balls about 3 inches apart on the cookie sheet (you do not need to grease the cookie sheet).

3 Dip the fork into a small amount of granulated sugar. Firmly press the fork in a crisscross pattern on the balls.

Bake 9 to 10 minutes or until the cookies are light brown. Use the pot holders to take cookie sheet out of oven. Cool cookies on cookie sheet for 2 minutes. Take cookies off cookie sheet, using the pancake turner, and put them on the wire cooling rack to finish cooling.

CHECK IT OUT!

If the dough is too soft to shape into balls, chill out! Cover the dough with plastic wrap, and put it in the refrigerator for about 1 hour.

NUTRITION INFORMATION

1 COOKIE: Calories 95 (Calories from Fat 45); Fat 5g (Saturated 1g); Cholesterol 6mg; Sodium 85mg; Carbohydrate 10g (Dietary Fiber 0g); Protein 2g

% DAILY VALUE: Vitamin A 2%; Vitamin C 0%; Calcium 0%; Iron 2%

DIET EXCHANGES: 1/2 Starch, 1 Fat

Funky Fudge

UTeNSiLS

Square pan, 8 x 8 inches
Pastry brush
Measuring cup
Medium saucepan
Wooden spoon
Can opener
Measuring spoons
Sharp knife

iNGReDieNTS

Margarine or butter (to grease pan)
  or aluminum foil
3 cups semisweet chocolate chips
1 can (14 ounces) sweetened
  condensed milk
1 teaspoon vanilla
1/8 teaspoon salt
Decorating icing (any color),
  if you like

1. Grease the pan with the **MARGARINE**, using the pastry brush, or line the pan with the aluminum foil. Save for later (you will need this in step 4).

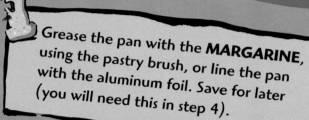

4. Pour the chocolate mixture into the greased pan. Spread evenly with the back of the spoon. Put pan of fudge in refrigerator for about 2 hours or until fudge is firm.

2. Put the **CHOCOLATE CHIPS** in the saucepan. Cook over low heat, stirring a few times with the wooden spoon, until chocolate chips are melted. Take saucepan off hot burner.

5. Cut the fudge into 8 rows by 4 rows, using the knife. Decorate fudge with **DECORATING ICING**, if you like. Cover any leftover fudge with plastic wrap or aluminum foil, and put it in the refrigerator.

3. Open the can of **SWEETENED CONDENSED MILK**, using the can opener. Add sweetened condensed milk, **VANILLA** and **SALT** to melted chocolate. Stir until mixed.

NUTRITION INFORMATION

1 PIECE Calories 135 (Calories from Fat 55); Fat 6g (Saturated 4g); Cholesterol 5mg; Sodium 30mg; Carbohydrate 20g (Dietary Fiber 1g); Protein 2g

% DAILY VALUE: Vitamin A 0%; Vitamin C 0%; Calcium 4%; Iron 2%

DIET EXCHANGES: 1 Starch, 1 Fat

Prep: Freeze: Makes:

15 minutes   **4¾** hours   **7** pops

Hip-Hop Frozen Pops

INGREDIENTS

1 can (8 ounces) crushed pineapple
2 cups vanilla yogurt
1 can (6 ounces) frozen orange
  juice concentrate, thawed

UTENSILS

Can opener
Strainer
Medium bowl
Measuring cup
Spoon
7 three-ounce paper cups
7 wooden ice-cream sticks with
  rounded ends

126

CHECK IT OUT!

You also can make these pops without the wooden sticks. Just peel off the paper cup as you eat the frozen pop.

1 Open the can of **PINEAPPLE** with the can opener. Pour pineapple into the strainer over the sink to drain. Put pineapple in the bowl.

2 Add the **YOGURT** and **ORANGE JUICE CONCENTRATE** to pineapple. Stir with the spoon until mixed.

3 Spoon the yogurt mixture into the paper cups. Put cups in the freezer for about 45 minutes or until mixture begins to thicken.

4 Poke a wooden stick into the center of each pop. Freeze for about 4 hours longer or until pops are hard. Before eating, peel the paper cups from the frozen pops.

NUTRITION INFORMATION

1 POP: Calories 140 (Calories from Fat 10); Fat 1g (Saturated 1g); Cholesterol 5mg; Sodium 40mg; Carbohydrate 29g (Dietary Fiber 0g); Protein 4g

% DAILY VALUE: Vitamin A 2%; Vitamin C 32%; Calcium 12%; Iron 0%

DIET EXCHANGES: 1 1/2 Fruit, 1/2 Skim Milk

PReP: Freeze. Makes:

 30 minutes **2** hours **8** servings

iNGReDieNTS

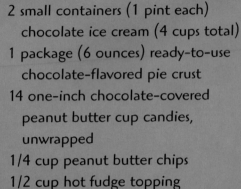

2 small containers (1 pint each) chocolate ice cream (4 cups total)

1 package (6 ounces) ready-to-use chocolate-flavored pie crust

14 one-inch chocolate-covered peanut butter cup candies, unwrapped

1/4 cup peanut butter chips

1/2 cup hot fudge topping

UTeNSiLS

Large spoon or ice-cream scoop
Plastic wrap
Measuring cups
Small spoon
Sharp knife

Sunken Treasure Ice-Cream Pie

1. Take 1 container of **ICE CREAM** out of the freezer. Put it on the counter for about 10 minutes or until ice cream is a little soft.

2. Spoon the softened ice cream into the **PIE CRUST**, using the large spoon or ice-cream scoop. Spread ice cream over pie crust, using the back of the spoon.

3. Put the **CANDIES** on top of ice cream layer. Cover pie with the plastic wrap and put in freezer for 1 hour.

4. Take the other container of ice cream out of the freezer. Put it on the counter for about 10 minutes or until the ice cream is a little soft.

5. Take the pie out of the freezer. Spoon softened ice cream over candy layer. Spread ice cream over candies, using the back of the spoon. Sprinkle the **PEANUT BUTTER CHIPS** over ice cream. Cover with plastic wrap and put back in freezer for 1 hour.

6. Take the pie out of the freezer. Drizzle **HOT FUDGE TOPPING** over top of pie, using the small spoon. Cut the pie into 8 slices, using the knife. Serve right away. Cover any leftover pie with plastic wrap, and put it in the freezer.

> This pie is like a Peanut Butter Sunken Treasure because of the peanut butter cup candies hidden in the ice cream.
>
> —CHRIS

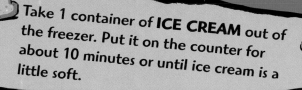

NUTRITION INFORMATION

1 SERVING: Calories 415 (Calories from Fat 205); Fat 23g (Saturated 11g); Cholesterol 30mg; Sodium 220mg; Carbohydrate 48g (Dietary Fiber 2g); Protein 6g

% DAILY VALUE: Vitamin A 6%; Vitamin C 0%; Calcium 10%; Iron 8%

DIET EXCHANGES: Not recommended

Make It! Shake It! Milk Shakes

UTeNSiLS

Measuring cups
Ice-cream scoop
Blender with lid
2 tall glasses
Straws

iNGReDieNTS

3/4 cup milk
1/4 cup chocolate-flavored syrup
3 large scoops vanilla ice cream
(about 1 1/2 cups total)

Here's another idea

Make a **COOKIES 'N' CREAM SHAKE**: Add 2 tablespoons crushed creme-filled chocolate sandwich cookies to the milk, chocolate syrup and ice cream before blending.

1 Put the **MILK, CHOCOLATE SYRUP** and **ICE CREAM** in the blender. Cover blender with lid, and blend on low speed about 10 seconds or until smooth.

2 Pour the shake into the glasses. Serve right away with the straws.

Here's another idea

Make a **CREAMY CARAMEL SHAKE**: Use 1/4 cup caramel topping instead of the chocolate syrup.

Here's another idea

Make a **MALTED MILK SHAKE**: Add 1/4 cup malted milk powder to the milk, chocolate syrup and ice cream before blending.

Here's another idea

Make a **DOUBLE CHOCOLATE SHAKE**: Use 3 large scoops chocolate ice cream instead of the vanilla ice cream.

NUTRITION INFORMATION

1 SERVING: Calories 345 (Calories from Fat 115); Fat 13g (Saturated 8g); Cholesterol 50mg; Sodium 160mg; Carbohydrate 50g (Dietary Fiber 1g); Protein 7g

% DAILY VALUE: Vitamin A 14%; Vitamin C 2%; Calcium 24%; Iron 4%

DIET EXCHANGES: Not recommended

CHAPTER 5

Where's it at?

PARTY TIME

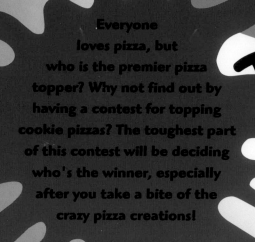

Everyone loves pizza, but who is the premier pizza topper? Why not find out by having a contest for topping cookie pizzas? The toughest part of this contest will be deciding who's the winner, especially after you take a bite of the crazy pizza creations!

PrizeWinning Pizza Party

EASY PARTY PLAN

Early in the day, make the pizza crust recipe for **TOPSY-TURVY COOKIE PIZZA** (page 136), but don't spread it in the pizza pan. Instead, shape the dough into 2-inch balls (they should be about the size of a golf ball). Put the balls on a cookie sheet, and press them into circles, using the back of a spoon. Bake at 350° for 8 to 10 minutes or until golden brown. Use potholders to take cookie sheet out of oven. Press the center of each cookie with the back of a spoon to make a crust. Cool on a wire cooling rack until cookies are no longer warm when touched.

Just before your friends come over, make the **CHOCOLATE PIZZA SAUCE** (page 136). Pick out a bunch of different toppings, and put them in separate bowls. Here are some topping ideas:

- Candy-coated chocolate candies
- Gummy bears or gummy worms candy
- Candy sprinkles
- Chopped nuts (such as pecans, peanuts, almonds)
- Colored sugar
- Shredded coconut
- Miniature marshmallows
- Miniature chocolate chips
- Jelly beans
- Gumdrops
- Broken pretzel sticks
- Candy corn
- Fresh fruit (such as banana or strawberry slices)
- Ice-cream toppings (such as chocolate or caramel)

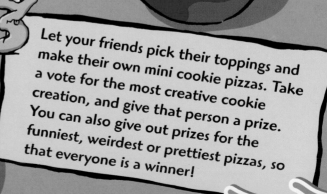

Let your friends pick their toppings and make their own mini cookie pizzas. Take a vote for the most creative cookie creation, and give that person a prize. You can also give out prizes for the funniest, weirdest or prettiest pizzas, so that everyone is a winner!

Turn the page

UTENSILS

Round pizza pan, 12 inches across
Pastry brush
Medium mixing bowl
Measuring cups
Measuring spoons
Wooden spoon
Pot holders
Wire cooling rack
Small saucepan
Small spatula
Pizza cutter or sharp knife

Topsy-Turvy Cookie Pizza

INGREDIENTS

Pizza Crust
Shortening (to grease pizza pan)
1 egg
1/2 cup packed brown sugar
1/4 cup granulated sugar
1/2 cup (1 stick) margarine or butter, soft enough to spread
1 teaspoon vanilla
1 1/4 cups all-purpose flour
1/2 teaspoon baking soda

Chocolate Pizza Sauce
1 bag (6 ounces) semisweet chocolate chips (1 cup)
2 tablespoons margarine or butter
3 tablespoons milk
1 cup powdered sugar

1/2 cup candy-coated chocolate candies

CHECK IT OUT!

Fool your friends with a sweet-tooth lover's pizza. Use red fruit leather that's been cut into 1-inch circles for "pepperoni," shredded coconut tinted with yellow food color for "cheese," cut-up red licorice and green gumdrops for "bell peppers," black gumdrops for "olives," and lemon slice candies for "pineapple."

1 Heat the oven to 350°. Grease the pizza pan with the **SHORTENING**, using the pastry brush. Save for later (you will need this in step 4).

2 Crack the **EGG** on side of the bowl, letting egg slip into bowl. Add the **BROWN SUGAR, GRANULATED SUGAR**, 1/2 cup **MARGARINE** and **VANILLA** to egg. Stir with the wooden spoon until mixed.

3 Add the **FLOUR** and **BAKING SODA** to sugar mixture. Stir until mixed (the dough will be stiff).

4 Spread or pat the dough in the greased pizza pan, using the back of the spoon or your hands.

5 Bake for about 15 minutes or until the crust is golden brown. Use the pot holders to take pan out of oven. Put pan on the wire cooling rack. Cool crust before spreading with sauce.

6 While the crust is cooling, make the **Chocolate Pizza Sauce** by putting the **CHOCOLATE CHIPS**, 2 tablespoons **MARGARINE** and **MILK** in the saucepan. Cook over low heat, stirring all the time with the wooden spoon, just until chocolate chips are melted. Take saucepan off hot burner.

7 Add the **POWDERED SUGAR** to chocolate mixture. Stir until smooth and shiny. Spread sauce over cooled crust, using the spatula.

8 Right away, sprinkle with the **CANDIES**. Cut the pizza into 16 slices, using the pizza cutter or knife.

Super-size this recipe by adding more candies on top!
—BEN

NUTRITION INFORMATION

1 SERVING: Calories 255 (Calories from Fat 110); Fat 12g (Saturated 4g); Cholesterol 15mg; Sodium 150mg; Carbohydrate 36g (Dietary Fiber 1g); Protein 2g

% DAILY VALUE: Vitamin A 10%; Vitamin C 0%; Calcium 2%; Iron 6%

DIET EXCHANGES: 2 Starch, 1/2 Fruit, 1 1/2 Fat

"Spooktacular" Halloween Party

Treat your friends to a creepy-crawly Halloween party. Looking for some fiendishly festive ideas? Try these hair-raising recipes guaranteed to give you goose bumps!

Bone-Chillin' Chili

Make a batch of **CHILL-CHASIN' CHILI** (page 78). You may want to double the recipe if you're inviting a lot of friends over. Instead of topping the chili with the shredded Cheddar cheese, cut slices of process **AMERICAN CHEESE** into Halloween shapes, using cookie cutters. Spoon the chili into bowls, and top with cheese shapes.

GREEN SLIME FRUIT DIP

Make **FANTASTIC FRUIT DIP** (page 46). Add a few drops of **GREEN FOOD COLOR** to give the dip a ghoulish glow. If you really want to freak out your friends, peel **RED** or **GREEN GRAPES** and poke a toothpick in each to make "eyeballs" and place around dip.

BRAIN JUICE

For a blood-curdling drink, add **RED CINNAMON CANDIES** to **HOT APPLE CIDER** and stir until melted.

Turn the page

SPIDER WEB CAKE

Make **COOKIES 'N' CREAM CAKE** (page 140). After the cake has cooled, frost it with vanilla frosting but don't top it with cookies. Instead, put **MELTED CHOCOLATE** or the extra chocolate frosting in a plastic bag with a zipper top. Seal the bag closed, and snip a small piece off the corner of the bag to make a writing tip. Squeeze the bag to make a small circle on the center of the cake with the chocolate. Make a larger circle around the small one. Keep doing this until you've made seven circles, one outside another. Right away, draw a knife through the frosting from the center of the cake to the outside. Do this around the cake six times, so the top of the cake looks like a spider web. Use a large **BLACK GUMDROP** and strings of skinny **BLACK LICORICE** to make a spider.

Boo!

139

Cookies

Utensils

Round cake pan, 8 or 9 inches across
Pastry brush
Measuring spoons
Cutting board
Small sharp knife
Large mixing bowl
Measuring cups
Electric mixer
Rubber scraper
Wooden spoon
Pot holders
Wire cooling rack
Table knife or small metal spatula

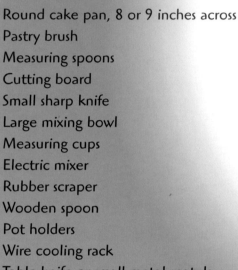

Ingredients

Shortening (to grease pan)
2 tablespoons all-purpose flour
    (to flour pan)
8 creme-filled chocolate sandwich
    cookies
1 egg
1 cup all-purpose flour
3/4 cup sugar
1/2 cup sour cream
1/4 cup (1/2 stick) margarine or
    butter, soft enough to spread
1/4 cup water
1/2 teaspoon baking soda
1/2 teaspoon baking powder
1 tub (16 ounces) vanilla or
    chocolate ready-to-spread
    frosting
Extra chocolate sandwich cookies,
    if you like

'n' Cream Cake

1 Heat the oven to 350°. Grease the pan with the **SHORTENING**, using the pastry brush.

2 Put the 2 tablespoons **FLOUR** in greased pan. Shake the pan to coat the bottom and sides with the flour, then pour out any extra flour. Save for later (you will need this in step 5).

3 Chop the 8 **COOKIES** into medium-size pieces on the cutting board, using the small sharp knife. Save for later (you will need them in step 5).

4 Crack the **EGG** on side of the bowl, letting egg slip into bowl. Add the 1 cup **FLOUR, SUGAR, SOUR CREAM, MARGARINE, WATER, BAKING SODA** and **BAKING POWDER** to egg. Beat with the electric mixer on low speed for 30 seconds. Turn off mixer. Scrape side of bowl with the rubber scraper, then beat on high speed for 2 minutes.

5 Add the chopped cookies to batter. Stir with the wooden spoon just until mixed. Pour batter into the greased and floured pan. Spread evenly with the rubber scraper.

6 Bake 30 to 35 minutes or until the cake springs back when touched lightly in center. Use the pot holders to take pan out of oven. Cool cake in pan for 10 minutes, then take cake out of pan and put on the wire cooling rack. Cool cake before frosting it.

1   2

3   4

7 Spread the **FROSTING** over the cake, using the table knife or spatula. (You might not use all of the frosting.) If you like, decorate cake with the extra **COOKIES**.

NUTRITION INFORMATION

1 SERVING: Calories 510 (Calories from Fat 180); Fat 20g (Saturated 11g); Cholesterol 40mg; Sodium 270mg; Carbohydrate 79g (Dietary Fiber 1g); Protein 4g

% DAILY VALUE: Vitamin A 10%; Vitamin C 0%; Calcium 4%; Iron 6%

DIET EXCHANGES: Not Recommended

141

Cookie SWAP!

Cookies—the only thing better than making them is eating them! Want to munch a bunch of different cookies? Why not invite some friends over for a cookie swap?

HERE'S WHAT TO DO

S Start by asking each of your friends to bring a batch of cookies to the party.

W When your friends arrive, put the cookies on plates, and set them on a table.

A Arrange boxes, containers or plastic plates and plastic bags.

P Pack up your favorite cookies and let everyone take some home.

SUPER SWAPPING COOKIES

- Rainbow Glitter Bars (page 118)
- Create-A-Cookie Tarts (page 144)
- Chocolate-Overload Brownies (page 116)
- Outrageous Candy Cookies (page 120)
- Peanutty Butter Cookies (page 122)

Hmmm... Have another favorite?

Awesome Cookie Art!

1 Make and bake a batch or two of **CREATE-A-COOKIE-TARTS** (page 144). Use different cookie cutters to make fun shapes.

Turn the page →

2 Invite friends over to frost and decorate the cookies. You can use any decorations you think are cool, such as candy sprinkles, crushed candies or colored sugar. Keep the frosting white or add a few drops of your favorite food color.

3 If you want to hang the cookies as decorations, poke a hole at the top of each cookie with the end of a plastic straw before you bake them. Then tie up with a string, ribbon or skinny licorice.

Create-A-Cookie Tarts

Large mixing bowl
Measuring cups
Measuring spoons
Wooden spoon
Rolling pin
Ruler, if you like
Round cookie cutter,
   3 inches across
Cookie sheet
Pot holders
Pancake turner
Wire cooling rack
Small mixing bowl
Spoon
Table knife or small
   metal spatula

INGREDIENTS

Cookies
1 egg
2 cups sugar
1 cup shortening
3/4 cup (1 1/2 sticks) margarine
   or butter, soft enough to spread
2 teaspoons vanilla
3 1/2 cups all-purpose flour
1 teaspoon baking powder
1/4 teaspoon salt
2 tablespoons all-purpose flour

Cream Cheese Frosting
1 package (8 ounces) cream
   cheese, soft enough to spread
1/2 cup sugar
1 teaspoon vanilla

Toppings (sliced fresh fruit,
   chopped nuts, small candy pie
   shredded coconut, candy sprinkles

CHECK IT OUT!

You can use different cookie cutter shapes and decorate these cookie tarts any way you like!

1 Heat the oven to 375°. Crack the **EGG** on side of the large bowl, letting egg slip into bowl. Add the 2 cups **SUGAR**, **SHORTENING**, **MARGARINE** and 2 teaspoons **VANILLA** to egg. Stir with the wooden spoon until mixed.

2 Add the 3 1/2 cups **FLOUR**, **BAKING POWDER** and **SALT** to sugar mixture. Stir until mixed. (If dough is very soft, cover it with plastic wrap and put it in the refrigerator for about 1 hour.)

3 Sprinkle the 2 tablespoons **FLOUR** over a clean surface (such as a kitchen counter or breadboard). Put dough on surface. Divide dough in half. Roll half of dough at a time, using rolling pin, until 1/4 inch thick. Use the ruler to measure, if you like.

4 Dip the cookie cutter into a small amount of flour, then cut the dough with the cookie cutter. Put cookies 2 inches apart on the cookie sheet (you do not need to grease the cookie sheet).

5 Bake 10 to 12 minutes or until the cookies are light brown. Use the pot holders to take cookie sheet out of oven. Cool cookies on cookie sheet for 1 minute. Take cookies off cookie sheet, using the pancake turner. Cool cookies on the wire cooling rack before frosting them.

6 While the cookies are cooling, make the **Cream Cheese Frosting** by putting the **CREAM CHEESE**, 1/2 cup **SUGAR** and 1 teaspoon **VANILLA** in the small bowl. Stir with the spoon until smooth and creamy.

7 Spread about 2 teaspoons of the frosting over each cookie, using the table knife or spatula. Top with your favorite **TOPPINGS**. Cover any leftover cookies with plastic wrap, and put them in the refrigerator.

NUTRITION INFORMATION

1 COOKIE: Calories 270 (Calories from Fat 145); Fat 16g (Saturated 5g); Cholesterol 15mg; Sodium 110mg; Carbohydrate 31g (Dietary Fiber 1g); Protein 2g

% DAILY VALUE: Vitamin A 8%; Vitamin C 6%; Calcium 2%; Iron 4%

DIET EXCHANGES: 2 Starch, 2 Fat

Camp-In Party

If the weather is too cold or rainy to camp out, why not have a "camp-in" party? Wondering what to pack? Try these ideas.

GOOD OL' GORP

GOOD OL' GORP (page 44) keeps you power-packed with energy. Make enough for your camping crew and put a handful or two into small plastic bags with zipper tops.

MELLOW-OUT HOT COCOA

Mellow-out with some hot cocoa. Here's a recipe that's as easy as 1-2-3.

 Put 3 tablespoons **SUGAR**, 3 tablespoons **BAKING COCOA**, 1/8 teaspoon **SALT** and 3/4 cup **WATER** in a saucepan. Stir with a wooden spoon until mixed. Heat over medium-high heat, stirring a few times, until water is boiling fast.

 Turn the heat down to low. Slowly add 2 1/4 cups **MILK**. Heat 2 to 3 minutes, stirring all the time, until cocoa is hot. (Be careful not to let the mixture boil.)

 Take the saucepan off hot burner. Carefully pour the hot cocoa into an insulated thermos or into 4 mugs. Top with **MARSHMALLOWS**, if you like.

CONFETTI HAM & CHEESE WRAPS

CONFETTI HAM & CHEESE WRAPS (page 62) make great portable sandwiches when you're in the "wild." Wrap 'em up in plastic wrap, and keep them cold if you won't be eating them for a while.

INDOOR S'MORES

There's no need to build a fire when you make **INDOOR S'MORES** (page 148). Wrap the bars in plastic wrap or aluminum foil, and you'll be set to go.

Turn the page

Pack all the food, some napkins and insulated cups in a picnic basket. Find a space in your house to spread a blanket on the floor. Grab a couple of flashlights, turn down the lights and share ghost stories with your friends.

Indoor S'mores

Rectangular pan, 13 x 9 inches
Plastic bag with zipper top
Measuring cups
Measuring spoons
Large saucepan
Wooden spoon
Sharp knife

INGREDIENTS

Cooking spray
12 graham cracker squares
3 cups milk chocolate chips
2 tablespoons peanut butter
3 cups miniature marshmallows

CHECK IT OUT!

In a sticky situation? If the marshmallows are sticking to the spoon like glue, try spraying the back of the spoon with a little cooking spray before you spread the gooey mixture in the pan.

1 Spray the pan with the **COOKING SPRAY**. Save for later (you will need this in step 4).

2 Put the **GRAHAM CRACKERS** in the plastic bag. Seal bag closed. Squeeze the bag until crackers are broken into small pieces. (The pieces should be about the size of a postage stamp.)

Spread the marshmallow mixture in the sprayed pan, using back of wooden spoon. Put pan of bars in the refrigerator for about 1 hour or until firm. Cut the pan of bars into 8 rows by 6 rows, using the knife. Wrap any leftover bars with plastic wrap, and put them back in the refrigerator.

It's fun to make this really easy recipe— just mix, chill and eat!
—BECKY

3 Put the **CHOCOLATE CHIPS** and **PEANUT BUTTER** in the saucepan. Cook over low heat, stirring all the time with the wooden spoon, until chocolate chips are melted. Take saucepan off hot burner. Stir in the graham cracker pieces and the **MARSHMALLOWS**.

NUTRITION INFORMATION

1 BAR: Calories 85 (Calories from Fat 35); Fat 4g (Saturated 2g); Cholesterol 5mg; Sodium 30mg; Carbohydrate 11g (Dietary Fiber 0g); Protein 1g

% DAILY VALUE: Vitamin A 0%; Vitamin C 0%; Calcium 2%; Iron 0%

DIET EXCHANGES: 1/2 Starch, 1 Fat

Cool Crafts

Easy Fun Dough

Remember, this dough is to play with, not to eat!

Stuff You'll Need

Measuring cups
Measuring spoons
4–cup microwavable measuring cup or large microwavable mixing bowl
Wooden spoon
Small mixing bowl
Rubber scraper
Spoon
Plastic bag with zipper top

1 1/4 cups Bisquick Original baking mix
1/4 cup salt
1 teaspoon cream of tartar
1 cup water
1 teaspoon food color (your favorite color)
2 tablespoons Bisquick Original baking mix

1 Put the 1 1/4 cups **BAKING MIX, SALT** and **CREAM OF TARTAR** in the microwavable measuring cup. Stir with the wooden spoon until mixed.

2 Put the **WATER** and **FOOD COLOR** in the small bowl. Stir the colored water into the dry mixture, a little at a time, until all the water is added. Microwave uncovered on High for 1 minute.

3 Scrape the mixture from the side of the measuring cup, using the rubber scraper, and stir with wooden spoon. Microwave uncovered on High 2 to 3 minutes, stopping every minute to stir, until the mixture almost forms a ball.

4 Put the measuring cup with the dough on the counter for 3 minutes.

5 Use a spoon to take the dough out of the measuring cup. Put dough on the counter for about 15 minutes or until cool enough to handle.

6 Sprinkle the 2 tablespoons **BAKING MIX** over a clean surface (such as a kitchen counter or breadboard). Put dough on surface. Knead dough by folding and pushing with the palms of your hands, then make a quarter turn. Repeat these steps to knead for about 1 minute or until dough is smooth. (If the dough is sticky, add 1 to 2 tablespoons of baking mix.)

7 Shape the dough into your favorite shapes and designs. Store dough in a plastic bag with zipper top in the refrigerator up to 2 weeks.

CHECK IT OUT!

Mix up your own fun dough to keep on hand for whenever the urge to create strikes. Try using different gadgets such as pinking shears, cookie cutters, a garlic press or a pizza roller to make designs and shapes. You can even turn them into decorations. Let your imagination run wild!

Squiggle Paint

Measuring cups
Measuring spoon
Medium mixing bowl
Spoon
Plastic squeeze bottle*

1/4 cup all-purpose flour
1/4 cup salt
1/4 cup water
2 tablespoons tempera powder
  (your favorite color)
Glitter, if you like

*Save squeeze bottles from ketchup, mustard, honey and other products.

1 Put the **FLOUR, SALT, WATER** and **TEMPERA POWDER** in the bowl. Stir with the spoon until well mixed. Pour paint into the bottle. Repeat this step with different tempera powders to make more colors.

2 Squeeze designs onto paper, cardboard or papier-mâché sculptures.

3 Right away, sprinkle the **GLITTER** over paint, if you like. Let dry. Store paint in a covered container at room temperature up to 5 days.

Papier-Mâché Bowl

Stuff You'll Need

Bowl (any size you like)
Measuring cups
Medium mixing bowl
Wire whisk
Ruler, if you like
Table knife
Paint brushes

Petroleum jelly
1 cup all-purpose flour
1 cup cold water
Newspaper, torn into about
  3 x 1-inch to 5 x 1-inch strips
Tempera paint (your favorite color)
Clear sealing spray for crafts, if you like

Remember, papier-mâché paste is to play with, not to eat!

4 Dip more newspaper strips into paste. Add a second layer of newspaper strips to bowl, putting them crosswise over the first layer of strips.

1 Put the bowl upside down. Spread a thick layer of **PETROLEUM JELLY** over the outside and rim of bowl.

2 Put the **FLOUR** and **WATER** in the mixing bowl. Beat with the wire whisk until smooth.

3 Dip 1 **NEWSPAPER STRIP** at a time into paste. Pull strip between 2 fingers to take off extra paste. Put wet newspaper strips on outside of bowl in an up-and-down pattern, covering all of bowl.

5 Dip more newspaper strips into paste. Add 4 more layers of newspaper strips to bowl, first going up and down, then going across. Let dry for 24 hours.

6 Take the papier-mâché bowl off the regular bowl, using the knife to loosen around the edge. Paint inside and outside of papier-mâché bowl with the **TEMPERA PAINT**. Let dry.

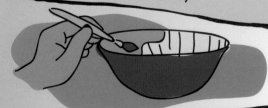

7 Spray the **SEALING SPRAY** on bowl to keep it longer. Store paste in a covered container in the refrigerator up to 5 days.

You Can Dough It!

Stuff You'll Need

Measuring cups
Large mixing bowl
Wooden spoon
Measuring spoon
Plastic wrap
Cookie sheet
Pot holders
Pancake turner
Wire cooling rack
Paint brushes

4 cups all-purpose flour
1 cup salt
1 1/2 cups warm water
Paste food color or tempera powder (your favorite color), if you like
2 tablespoons all-purpose flour
Tempera paint or watercolors, if you like
Clear sealing spray for crafts, if you like

1 Heat the oven to 300°. Put the 4 cups **FLOUR** and **SALT** in the bowl. Stir with the wooden spoon until well mixed. Stir in the **WARM WATER**. Stir in the **FOOD COLOR** or **TEMPERA POWDER**, if you like.

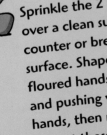

2 Sprinkle the 2 tablespoons **FLOUR** over a clean surface (such as a kitchen counter or breadboard). Put dough on surface. Shape dough into a ball, using floured hands. Knead dough by folding and pushing with the palms of your hands, then make a quarter turn. Repeat these steps to knead 5 to 10 minutes or until dough is smooth and elastic. Wrap dough tightly in the plastic wrap.

3 Take out only as much dough as you will use at one time because dough dries out quickly. Use the dough to make fun shapes.

4 Put the shapes on the cookie sheet. Bake for about 1 hour or until dough is dry and just begins to brown. The bake time will depend on size of shapes. If more bake time is needed, turn shapes over and continue baking until dough is dry.

5 Use the pot holders to take cookie sheet out of oven. Take shapes off cookie sheet, using the pancake turner, and put them on the wire cooling rack. Cool shapes before painting.

6 Paint the shapes with the **TEMPERA PAINT** or **WATERCOLORS**, if you like. Spray the **SEALING SPRAY** on shapes to keep them longer. Store unbaked dough tightly wrapped in the refrigerator up to 30 days.

Here's another idea

Make a necklace: For the beads, shape some of the dough into about 1-inch balls. Push a toothpick through each bead to make a hole. Bake and cool beads. Paint the beads, then string them on heavy thread or cord. To keep each bead in place, tie a knot in the thread on each side of the bead.

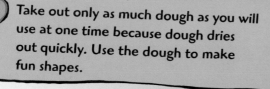

HELPFUL NUTRITION AND COOKING INFORMATION

NUTRITION GUIDELINES

We provide nutrition information for each recipe that includes calories, fat, cholesterol, sodium, carbohydrate, fiber and protein. Individual food choices can be based on this information.

Recommended intake for a daily diet of 2,000 calories as set by the Food and Drug Administration:

Total Fat	Less than 65g
Saturated Fat	Less than 20g
Cholesterol	Less than 300mg
Sodium	Less than 2,400mg
Total Carbohydrate	300g
Dietary Fiber	25g

CRITERIA USED FOR CALCULATING NUTRITION INFORMATION

- The first ingredient was used wherever a choice is given (such as 1/3 cup sour cream or plain yogurt).
- The first ingredient amount was used wherever a range is given (such as 3 to 3 1/2 pound cut-up broiler-fryer chicken).
- The first serving number was used wherever a range is given (such as 4 to 6 servings).
- "If desired" ingredients (such as sprinkle with brown sugar, if desired) and recipe variations were not inclued.
- Only the amount of a marinade or frying oil that is estimated to be absorbed by the food during preparation or cooking was calculated.

INGREDIENTS USED IN RECIPE TESTING AND NUTRITION CALCULATIONS

- Ingredients used for testing represent those that the majority of consumers use in their homes: large eggs, 2% milk, 80% lean ground beef, canned ready-to-use chicken broth, and vegetable oil spread containing not less than 65 percent fat.
- Fat-free, low-fat or low-sodium products are not used, unless otherwise indicated.
- Solid vegetable shortening (not butter, margarine, nonstick cooking sprays or vegetable oil spread as they can cause sticking problems) is used to grease pans, unless otherwise indicated.

EQUIPMENT USED IN RECIPE TESTING

We use equipment for testing that the majority of consumers use in their homes. If a specific piece of equipment (such as a wire whisk) is necessary for recipe success, it will be listed in the recipe.

- Cookware and bakeware without nonstick coatings were used, unless otherwise indicated.
- No dark colored, black or insulated bakeware was used.
- When a baking pan is specified in a recipe, a metal pan was used; a baking dish or pie plate means oven-proof glass was used.
- An electric hand mixer was used for mixing only when mixer speeds are specified in the recipe directions. When a mixer speed is not given, a spoon or fork was used.

THE FOOD GUIDE PYRAMID

The Food Guide Pyramid is your road map for planning your meals and snacks. It will help you choose the foods you should eat the most of to keep you feeling great.

The Food Guide Pyramid is divided into six parts, or food groups. To eat well, you want to start at the bottom of the pyramid and work your way up. At the bottom of the pyramid is the Bread, Cereal, Rice and Pasta Group. Most of the foods you eat in a day should come from this group. Foods that have a lot of calories but not many of the vitamins and minerals your body needs are at the very top of the pyramid. This group is called the Fats, Oils and Sugars Group. You should try to eat less from this group and more from the other groups in the pyramid.

Below the name of each food group are some numbers that tell you how many servings to eat from that group each day. At each meal, try to eat foods from at least three different food groups.

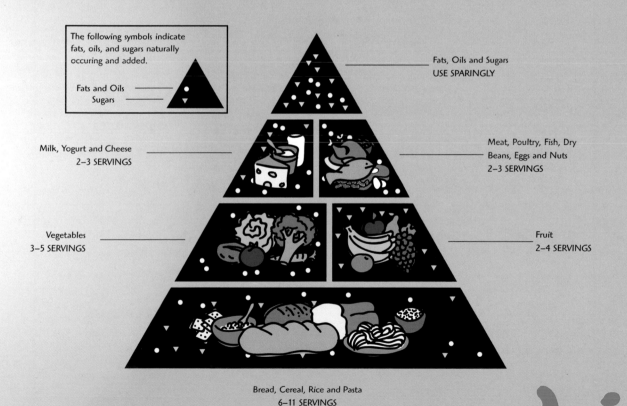

The following symbols indicate fats, oils, and sugars naturally occuring and added.

Fats and Oils ——— ○ ·
Sugars ——— ▽

Fats, Oils and Sugars
USE SPARINGLY

Milk, Yogurt and Cheese
2–3 SERVINGS

Meat, Poultry, Fish, Dry Beans, Eggs and Nuts
2–3 SERVINGS

Vegetables
3–5 SERVINGS

Fruit
2–4 SERVINGS

Bread, Cereal, Rice and Pasta
6–11 SERVINGS

Source: U.S. Department of Agriculture. U.S. Department of Health and Human Services.

METRIC CONVERSION GUIDE

Volume

U.S. Units	Canadian Metric	Australian Metric
1/4 teaspoon	1 mL	1 ml
1/2 teaspoon	2 mL	2 ml
1 teaspoon	5 mL	5 ml
1 tablespoon	15 mL	20 ml
1/4 cup	50 mL	60 ml
1/3 cup	75 mL	80 ml
1/2 cup	125 mL	125 ml
2/3 cup	150 mL	170 ml
3/4 cup	175 mL	190 ml
1 cup	250 mL	250 ml
1 quart	1 liter	1 liter
1 1/2 quarts	1.5 liters	1.5 liters
2 quarts	2 liters	2 liters
2 1/2 quarts	2.5 liters	2.5 liters
3 quarts	3 liters	3 liters
4 quarts	4 liters	4 liters

Weight

U.S. Units	Canadian Metric	Australian Metric
1 ounce	30 grams	30 grams
2 ounces	55 grams	60 grams
3 ounces	85 grams	90 grams
4 ounces (1/4 pound)	115 grams	125 grams
8 ounces (1/2 pound)	225 grams	225 grams
16 ounces (1 pound)	455 grams	500 grams
1 pound	455 grams	1/2 kilogram

Note: The recipes in this cookbook have not been developed or tested using metric measures. When converting recipes to metric, some variations in quality may be noted.

Measurements

Inches	Centimeters
1	2.5
2	5.0
3	7.5
4	10.0
5	12.5
6	15.0
7	17.5
8	20.5
9	23.0
10	25.5
11	28.0
12	30.5
13	33.0

Temperatures

Fahrenheit	Celsius
32°	0°
212°	100°
250°	120°
275°	140°
300°	150°
325°	160°
350°	180°
375°	190°
400°	200°
425°	220°
450°	230°
475°	240°
500°	260°

Index

NOTE: *Italicized* page numbers indicate a photograph.